WHISPERS

OF THE SHEPHERD

Destiny Image® Publishers, Inc.
Shippensburg, PA

Y. M. TIKKUN

WHISPERS
OF THE SHEPHERD

DESTINY IMAGE® PUBLISHERS, INC.
P.O. Box 310, Shippensburg, PA 17257-0310

"We Publish the Prophets"

This book and all other Destiny Image, Revival Press, MercyPlace, Fresh Bread, Destiny Image Fiction, and Treasure House books are available at Christian bookstores and distributors worldwide.

For a U.S. bookstore nearest you, call 1-800-722-6774.

For more information on foreign distributors, call 717-532-3040.

Or reach us on the Internet: www.destinyimage.com

Library of Congress Cataloging-in-Publication Data

Tikkun, Y. M.
    Whispers of the Shepherd / by Y.M. Tikkun.
        p. cm.
      ISBN-10: 0-7864-2334-1
      ISBN-13: 978-0-7684-2334-1 (pbk. : alk. paper)
      I. Meditations.   I. Title.
  BV4811.T55 2006
  242--dc22

                                                      2005031576

For Worldwide Distribution, Printed in the U.S.A.

1 2 3 4 5 6 7 8 / 12 11 10 09 08 07 06

DEDICATION

This work is dedicated to the one true Shepherd, for truly the credit for this book belongs solely to Him. As I have been privileged to be a mere scribe of His inspirations in parable form, He alone must be considered the Author. Thanks be to God for His great love and for His breathed Word to His children. Truly God is with us, as He has been since the beginning.

Acknowledgments

With deep love and appreciation, I would like to acknowledge those who have covered this book with their many prayers. These same people have affirmed and encouraged me—a lowly scribe—confirming the true Authorship of *Whispers of the Shepherd*. I am greatly thankful to the God of Israel for His gift to me of a godly husband, who enabled me to travel to Jerusalem to receive the inspirations I've recorded in this book. Likewise, I am grateful for and blessed by my four children, who have sacrificed individually, so I might be able to take the time I needed to be away in order to listen to the Shepherd's whispers.

Special thanks must be given, likewise, to John and Aileen, who sheltered me and kept me in their home in Jerusalem. Their servanthood, love, and encouragement freed me to receive what the Lord offered.

Finally, I lift up praise and thanksgiving to God for Lee, my sister, who no longer dwells upon the earth. She prayed for this book as it was being written, but she died before its completion. In life she, too, heard quiet whispers from her Shepherd. Now, fully in His presence, she not only hears Him, but speaks to Him face to face.

Special thanks to Barbara Hogan for her typing and formatting of the manuscript in English. Her hours of love and care brought the pages of these parables into the place where dreams are realized. She became a selfless answer to prayer in God's perfect timing.

A special word of thanks and praise must be offered up to the Shepherd for Florence, as well. At a time when her life was filled with challenges and uncertainty, she was able to hear the voice of the Shepherd calling her to sow into the production of this book with financial "seeds." This was a profound act of faith and love, as well as obedience on her part. I pray for her to receive a thousand fold blessing for this precious sacrifice to Him. Florence, your mother is now in personal dialogue with the Shepherd of Israel.

For the many people who served as advisors, proofreaders, encouragers, and supporters in numerous ways, I am humbly grateful. Without the prayer support of so many people and without the encouragement of other sheep in the Shepherd's flock, this book may never have found its way into print.

ENDORSEMENTS

Whispers of the Shepherd offers some incredible and thought-provoking insight. In fact, some of the insight is so deep and profound it could only come out of many hours of deep meditation in the prayer closet. You will be blessed and inspired as you read this book.

Jonathan Bernis
President of Jewish Voice Ministries International
and host of "Jewish Voice Today" weekly television program

Whispers of the Shepherd is a compelling journey into the presence of the Lord that will minister Life to the most seasoned believer and non-believing seeker alike. Classic devotionals like *My Utmost for His Highest* and *Streams in the Desert* provoke thought based on deep revelation of truth. *Whispers of the Shepherd* goes beyond the intellect with words that are Spirit to spirit. This unique devotional carries an aura of timeless wisdom. Its rich savor is worthy of multiple readings.

Morris Ruddick
President, Global Initiatives Foundation
Executive Director, Strategic Intercession Global Network
Author, *God's Economy, Israel and the Nations*

TABLE OF CONTENTS

"THE WORDS OF THE WISE
ARE LIKE GOADS, THEIR COLLECTED
SAYINGS LIKE FIRMLY EMBEDDED NAILS—
GIVEN BY ONE SHEPHERD."

(ECCLES. 12:11, NIV).

"ב . ר . י ח ָ כ ָ מ ִ י ָ ר ְ ב נ ת ,

כ ָ מ ָ מ ְ ר ת נ ְ ט ע ִ י ָ ע ֻ ל ֵ י א ֻ ס ת ;

מ ֵ ר ' ע ֶ ה א ֶ ח ָ ד , ב ֻ נ ָ ."

ב יא" קוהלת י.

REFLECTIONS

Little one, look at the quiet mountain lake, serving as a mirror for the mountain. The reflection is a perfect match of the reality, but it is upside down. Are there really clouds in the water, and spiry peaks descending into the lake? No! But in the reflection, it appears that there are.

In the world of the spirit, the realities are quite different from what you see in the natural. Things in the natural are the reflection of spiritual things, even as the mountain lake reflects the clouds and mountains. The things of My Kingdom, when reflected, appear to be upside down to natural human understanding.

What appears as weakness to the world may well be true Kingdom strength. What appears to be worldly gain is Kingdom loss. Often, what appears as holy and acceptable to the world is unholy and unacceptable to Me.

What, then, is the true reality? Is it the mountain or its reflection? Of course it is the mountain. My Kingdom and My ways are the mountain. The ways of men are but a reflection. Which has substance and which will endure? As soon as a storm moves upon the surface of the water, the reflection vanishes. The mountain, however, will remain.

The evil in the world today would appear to be overcoming the good. The weight and pain of that perception become a crushing force to the human heart. But those who dwell in My heart never lose. As the world depletes, My Spirit repletes. However, this law applies only for those who dwell within My Kingdom. For those who insist on clinging to the reflection—the world's perspective—their losing will be real in both realms.

I have shown the way to the mountain, yet so many reject My Kingdom way as foolishness. Some see it as optional. Some see it as negotiable, picking and choosing which parts of the two realities are to be blended together in order to make life palatable. Is truth ever negotiable? No! Truth simply *is*! The way of the world is to make truth an individual determination. What foolishness! Try to climb the mountain that you see reflected in the lake! If one's folly in attempting this ascent is not soon discovered, the "mountain climber" will most certainly drown. Surely, I have not left the world without this truth and without this understanding. My Word is clear. The example of the Messiah has been perfectly placed before humankind.

So, why does the deception continue? Why do My children live in opposition to My truth? They have believed the lies of My enemy, the great deceiver. They act out their errant choices, and thereby they bring pain and suffering upon each other. From a human point of view, I should end it all now. Indeed, I should crush the deceiver, or perhaps I should never have allowed him to have such a position of power. These words speak out of the reflection, not out of the truth. I know truths about the nature of creation that you can not know. I know the deeper realities of the spirit that humans have only guessed at and have groped for unsuccessfully.

Truly, the lake will dry up when the fire falls upon it. The mountain, however, will stand in eternity. Do not live by the realities of the world. Do not cling to the understanding of the human mind, for these earthly pools will evaporate quickly. Do not judge My love and My truth by what you see in history. Judge them only by My Word and by My Spirit as you embrace the One who came to show the way to the Kingdom; in this way you will embrace the mountain.

Come, walk upon My mountain. Come up out of the lake of the world and walk upon holy ground. If you do so, you will grow in the knowledge of the truth. Your eyes will come to understand the reality of the reflection. Your judgments will be holy, but they will not be complete in truth, for no one in My human creation can know all truth. It was never meant for you to be able to do so in this life.

Where do you wish to dwell, little one? Do you wish to dwell upon the mountain or in the lake? Know that to live in Kingdom reality while living in flesh will be costly to you. You will be thought of as a fool. You will be battered and slandered, but do not lose sight of the reflection truth. What the world calls foolishness is, in truth, wisdom. What the world dishes out as battering to My Kingdom children is actually a building process for them. What the world sees as slander is high praise on My holy mountain. What the world sees as death is, in fact, life to My own. What appears to be neglect may be the focus of My greatest attention.

Must you know all things in order to be at peace with Me? All that you need has been made available to you. If you cannot see, ask for new vision and you will receive. If you require proof of My truth and of My reality, ask for faith, and I shall give it to you freely. Ask Me to meet your expectation, and you will see only *reflections*.

SHOES AND BARE FEET

Precious bare feet! How wonderful it is to walk in the early morning grass and feel the cool dew upon your bare feet. I designed the seashore—the water's edge—to be a delight to your toes as you wade in the surf.

And yet, some terrains are too harsh for the touch of bare feet. For comfort or protection, shoes, sandals, and boots are often necessary. But, as much comfort as shoes might provide, they also may produce great discomfort if they are not properly fitted.

If shoes are far too small, they may simply not be useful at all. If they are only slightly too small and are forced upon the feet, cramping or crippling can result. In such a case, a wince of pain may come with each step.

Problems can come from shoes that are too big, as well. While oversized shoes may be chosen in expectation of new growth to come, too much room inside the shoes can cause tripping, stumbling, and falling. Shoes, which fit too loosely can, additionally, cause painful rubbing, which may cause sores and blisters to emerge. Occasionally, during a sprint or a chase, a runner wearing such shoes may actually run out of the shoes completely.

Leaving one's protection behind and running in haste with no protection is always a serious danger!

Consider the spiritual implications of shoes, little one. In truth, I created My children to walk in purity with Me—with their feet uncovered, barefooted. The sin of the world has destroyed the freedom within My once safe world, replacing it with harshness and hazards.

Never forget that I have provided spiritual footwear for you, My child. I have provided this so that you may walk in this world with protection and certainty. I have given you My Word and have provided you with spiritual understanding. Those who do not put on this protection, however, will wince and cry out as they take each step upon the world's harsh terrain. Others will try to put on just a bit of protection, wishing to find out only what they can perceive of the world's truth. They choose their own understanding of My Word. They walk upon stunted feet with their toes curled under.

Still others see the need for protection. However, they want to take their journey with the biggest possible steps. They want to put shoes that are too big upon their "spiritual feet." Rather than allowing themselves to grow properly, step by step and size by size, they seek to become spiritual giants and end up with shoes that are too big for their feet to fill.

Such people cannot maneuver well on their spiritual journey. They trip and fall as they tackle the hazards of life with concepts that are too big for their understanding.

It is good to be a warrior in spiritual warfare, but one must grow into that calling. To tackle the dark world with spiritually tiny feet in shoes that are too big can be very dangerous, indeed. The greatest danger would be walking out of the spiritual shoes—out of the protection altogether. Even if the feet remain in the shoes that are too large, there will be needless rubbing and friction.

Too much room in which to maneuver is dangerous for My little ones.

My Word and My instruction perfectly cling to those who journey upon this earth. My word and My instruction must support the developing structures and protect them from all dangers. I know exactly what size you are, and, therefore, I know exactly what you need. I know when you have filled out a place in your spiritual journey—in your spiritual growth—and when you are ready for the next size. Do not try to leap ahead in your growth process, and don't try to stay back either, clinging to the naive, safe past of a smaller size.

You were created for growth, but you were not created to grow without protection and guidance. I will supply all that you need. Do not go into areas to which I have not called you, and don't enter areas beyond your growth and understanding. Do not try to go barefooted on the journey, without My Word or instruction.

Do not run ahead in shoes that are too big and thereby lose and leave behind that which I have provided for your safety. Truly, I say to you that someday you will again walk with Me in bare feet. When that time comes, there will be no hazards. Your growth, your understanding, and your intimacy with Me will be complete. Until then, wear the shoes I have provided for you and have fitted to your feet. In them you will be safe, and you will be free to grow toward the season of free feet in the dew and in the tender grass of My new morning in My new Kingdom.

Until then I need for you to keep your course on the journey I've assigned to you in the way I've ordained and in the supply I've provided. Do not scorn what I have designed for you, and do not argue against it. Simply walk. Walk in the joy of the journey. Walk in the victory I have promised to you. Run as I direct. Wear your footwear gratefully, for I crafted it especially and specifically for you out of My love for you. Do not compare your steps to those of any of My other children. What I have done for them is in accordance to My wisdom and My will for them just as what I've done for you is in accordance with My will for you.

Now, close your eyes. In this quiet moment of My love, remove your shoes. With your feet bare before Me, begin to dance. Dance with Me, little one. Before the time to return to your shoes, *dance* in My love. Truly I shall be dancing with you.

TENDER SEARCHING

Little one, the mountains were carved by My fingers generations ago. In each curve of their slopes—in each rise and fall—I have carved beauty and purpose. What is the purpose of these things? I carved them for majesty. I carved them for love and for strength. I carved them to speak of Me. I am mighty and yet I am near. I am awesome and yet I am soft. I am formless and yet I am formed.

Look upon Me, beloved, as you look upon these mountains. Look at Me with love and with the unity you feel with Me and with My strength in these moments. See the toil of the climb and the victory of the completed ascent. Touch them with your heart and soul, even as you "touch" them with your eyes.

See in them the shades and shadows of contrast. The darkness is most visible when it is held against the light. What lies within the folds of the mountains, deep within their hidden crevices? I know the beauty and the treasure that may be found there. I see the tiny waterfalls and the quiet streams. I see the spider's web and the monkey's nest.

What lies hidden in the crevices of those precious children who live without My light, little one? Seek My hidden treasure. Tenderly search for it. Love this hidden treasure before you are able to perceive it, even when it is unseen. Search for it, it will always be there.

Make your journey lovingly into those crevices without crushing the tender blades. I am there, My love. Will you venture there to find Me?

POOLS AND POPPIES

Come and sit beside My pool, little one. Shall I stir the water of life for you? Shall I change its color to entice you to dip into its waters? The pool of living water awaits you. Why do you hesitate to venture into its depths? Does your pain cause you to be afraid of changing position? Do you fear going deeper? Does your crippling condition make you doubt My promised healing? Rather than being disappointed, feeling rejected, or accepting a sense of failure, do you sit and wait?

What is the cost of entering My pool? The price is faith. Ask Me and I shall give you the quantity of faith that is needed to buy your entry into My pool. Are you too weak to step into this water? Do not ask others to bring you to the water's edge; instead, ask Me to bring the water to you.

Still you hesitate. Why? Perhaps you resist because entering into the water's blessing will change your life for all eternity. Those things that have been comfortable and familiar will be replaced by things untested and unproven in your life.

There is risk in change, you say. Yes, there is, but there is greater risk in remaining dry and broken in hope.

Miracles are what you need! They come to give proof that I still exist and that I do care. Do you not see miracles all around you? In a single glance you can observe hundreds of them. Do you not see them?

For example, look at the simple poppies. How is it that they sprout where they do? From barren rocks they spring forth in riots of color. Who was their planter and gardener? Notice how they hide from one season to the next. Who plans their scheduled time of fertility, rest, and blooming? I am the hand that put a vast ocean of flowers within the case of a single seed.

For generations a seed can remain dormant. Then, in a time of My choosing, nourished by that which I placed within it unseen growth begins. That which had been sleeping awakens. All the features of the flower—its color, its shape, its texture, and its fragrance—have been wrapped up in a single seed, awaiting My call to bring forth the miracle of life that exists within it.

Do I care for seeds? Do I plan for small details such as poppy seeds? Yes, I care for all things, especially things of new growth. How can the poppies viewed by Solomon's eyes be seen now by you? It is by the miracle of the seed and by the miracle of the pool of water that I have provided for them.

If I weave such miracles into poppies, why would I not weave many within you? You are the seed of My love, now blooming in its chosen time. Would you deny this?

Look again into the pool. See your face reflected there. It is unique to you and yet the substance of bone and flesh is the same as that material divinely chosen to enwrap your Messiah. Therefore, if this was a sufficient garment for Him, your physical body made of similar chemistry must then be a robe of honor for you to possess the same characteristics He has.

So, arise and enter My pool. Embrace the miracle of life that has been placed within you. Even as the poppy seed must yield itself up to change, for it must break through its shell and draw strength from the water of life, so must you. Therefore, step in. Believe. Risk.Change. Bloom. You are My miracle. So, bloom!

THE HEARTBEAT

Listen to the tick of the clock. Each tick is another moment of life passing by that shall never be recaptured. Do photographs and video images save the moment forever? No, they preserve only the recollection of the moment.

Similarly, every heartbeat is the tick of an eternal clock—of a moment lost—never to return. Why, then, do My children continually waste these precious seconds—these heartbeats—on vacant and empty things? Why do they allow them to pass by with no meaning and with no gain? They appear to be incidental, so they are ignored. How many heartbeats bring fruit to the soul? How many heartbeats bring life to the physical body only, while bringing slow death to the spirit?

The heartbeat is an eternal clock. It not only measures life in this world, but it also measures the life in the world to come. Each beat is designed to add to eternity—to Kingdom gain. Each beat is precious and significant.

I do not mean for this truth to be a bondage to you. Do not allow it to become a source of anxiousness or drivenness within your soul; I mean this revelation to be a gift for your gain, for joy, and for lasting purpose.

If there was to be a fixed and limited supply of water upon the earth, would you allow for one drop to be wasted? How precious each drop would be in your sight! Then, why waste a single heartbeat? Each person has only a fixed and limited number and no more.

Do not cling to each heartbeat as if seeking to possess it. Give each one to Me, that I might possess them all. I can bring an abundance from them that you have never dreamed possible. And each one that is placed in My hand shall be an eternal reality that will live forever.

Too many heartbeats have passed by without notice. Too many have been possessed by empty leisure. Too many have been given to My enemy for his accumulation and accounting. Begin anew! Begin now to give each heartbeat to Me. I shall keep them well, and I shall return to you their collection as a glorious, eternal inheritance.

GIFTED DUCKS

Behold the ducks, little one. Behold these buoyant inhabitants of the lake. See how they spend their day. What is their joy? What is their priority? What is their purpose? To skim across the surface of the water with little effort would seem to be a thrill through human eyes. But, these gifted swimmers see such a gift as a matter of natural course. They do not consciously celebrate it.

They use this gift with little attention given to it. Yet, it truly *is* a gift. Every detail of their bodies has been carefully planned to help them use this gift. Every stroke of their feet, every drop of oil on their feathers, and every air pocket within their bodies was perfectly and intentionally engineered by Me.

What about you is a gifting from Me, little one? What do you see as a matter of course, something that is taken for granted? Is it your ability to speak? How freely I give this gift, yet so few see it as a treasure. What is the treasure that is represented by this gift of speaking so that others can hear and understand? With speech, one can declare his or her state of need, joy, or desire. Through this gift one can become part of the life and journey of another person in an intimate and detailed way.

Understanding often comes through an exchange of spoken words in the same way learning does. What if I created My children to be silent? How different life would be! The exchange of thought could then occur only by non-verbal means. The written word could be used to speak, but how much more slowly? Does emotion translate as well or as accurately through non-verbal means? What harm often comes from emotions that are acted out, rather than spoken! What pain is often caused by this!

I created the heart, the mouth, and the brain to be connected. All three parts make a whole. All three form a gifting known as the spoken word. Are those of My children who lack this gift less gifted or less acceptable? No! I choose other gifts for them—gifts of great value.

Each of My children is deeply gifted. However, each must see that which has been bestowed as a true gift. These blessings must never be considered as demanded, rightful, expected, or casual things.

I have gifted all of My creation! Open your eyes to see the precious gifts I've given to you and others. What do you do with ease? What do you allow to be a matter of course in your life? Do you consider it foolish to appreciate the blinking of an eye, a sneeze, the ability to jump, or the capability to give a hug as a gift from Me? See everything through more inspired eyes. You are surrounded with a multitude of opportunities for rejoicing and yet your heart remains dull.

If you could swim in the way a duck does, you would be seen as truly gifted. If one of My little ducks were able to use words to demand the morsel of bread that may be hidden in your pocket, you would say that he was a truly an extraordinarily gifted little duck. Why not look upon those things which I have given to each of you as unique treasures? Apply these gifts wisely. Celebrate them! The joy and meaning of your life will thereby be expanded. Awaken from your dullness and *see!*

With each gift I give, a responsibility comes to use it wisely and faithfully. See to this! In doing so, you will taste deeper joy and understanding by knowing who I have created you to be. I love you, gifted little one!

KITTENS

Out of the quietness of the morning comes the gentle, persistent meowing of kittens. These little ones are so tiny that they are hidden away by their mother-protector. Why do they give away their presence by their tiny voices? Have they not been warned to remain silent? What in them would cause this violation of safe silence by revealing their sweet sounds? The mother has left them briefly, to find food. They are cold, lonely, and frightened.

What if she would never return? Who would then fill the deep emptiness caused by her absence? Who would fill the emptiness caused by hunger in their bellies and the void arising from the lack of their mother's touch or caress? These little ones know of only one source of life and comfort. When they sense that it is gone, they cry out even if it dangerous for them to do so. Soon sadness and sleepiness overtake them, and they curl closely together for warmth and companionship. Yet, they cannot give each other the food they long for—the food that is needed to fill their bellies.

Now, however, the kittens begin to cry again. They cry louder than before, but this time they cry in excitement. Why? Their mother is coming! They know she is nearby. Safety has returned to them. Again there are quiet kittens. Now they are warm, bathed by a loving tongue and fed by sweet milk. They sleep again in quiet rest.

How like a kitten you are, My child. You long for the presence of the One who gave you life. You desperately need the food that only I can give to you, and you desire My warm presence and safety. Unlike the mother cat, who needs to leave her little ones behind in order to sustain herself and them, I, Abba, will never leave you.

For you to mature, I need for you to grow, to open your eyes, and yet not be away from your perpetual dependence upon Me.

How I long for you to cry out because of the sense of distance that exists between you and Me—space that you have created by exploring life by your design and in your own way. Sometimes kittens do stray. They meet with danger in their too-eager independence. If two should wander away together when they are too young to return unaided, they will cling to each other, sustaining their hearts with the illusion that their mother is near. In their own touch and heartbeats they imagine that she is near.

Like curious kittens, My children wander away from Me, as well. In their desperate need to feel safe and loved again, they cling to each other. The illusion falls upon them that perhaps they, themselves, are the God they long for. How soon they can become weak, sick, and starved as a result of this illusion. It may even lead to death. If lost kittens cry out, their mother will come and carry them to their home nest again. If My little ones would cry out to Me, I would do the same.

Sometimes kittens get so lost in their fascination with the world and with the joy of play that they again lose sight of safety. Similarly, My children become preoccupied with the things and pleasures of this life in the form of possessions and leisure time. They wander out from their haven of My protection. Do I ever cease watching them with a loving eye? Do I ever fall ignorant of their location and activities? No!

Unlike the mother cat, I always know everything concerning you. In fact, I am ever watching you. When you are helpless and unknowing as if in infancy like a little kitten, I will move you away from danger. As you grow, My voice cries out to you in order to call you back from your wanderings.

Unlike kittens, I allow you time to grow up, but I never abandon you to your own destiny. I never withdraw My nourishment and say, "Seek your own elsewhere." I do give you freedom to refuse My food and My counsel, however. I do give you freedom, but even in your advanced years, you remain My little one whose cry I will always answer. I come. I lift up. I protect. In My presence you are fed and warmed. In My presence you will always have a constant companion keeping you from loneliness. In My presence you are empowered to be about the work I have given you to do. You will always have My presence with you.

I love you, little one. Come and nuzzle close to Me. Come and play with Me. Come and feed upon Me.

Know My love and My safety. I never suffocate My little ones by holding them too close. I never abandon My children. I always hear your tiniest cry whether it's in the silence or in the clamor of daily living. Come closer to Me.

HOURS, MINUTES, SECONDS

What makes up your day, little one? Is it one block of time added to another, hour added to hour? Is your day made up of tiny pieces called minutes, which seem to fly by at too great a rate? Or is your day lived out, second by second? Never forget that your day is a very precious commodity.

What price would a person pay to have one day added to his life? And yet, people walk or run through their days, as if those moments in time are inconsequential and disposable. They hardly even notice that a day has passed. They seem to notice only the events before them or their accomplished tasks. Only when they look at a calendar do they realize that a single day, or perhaps many have slipped away.

It is not My plan to have you see activities throughout a day without seeing the day itself. The many activities make the day a blur of activity. Some would like to see the day end early so that the stress it has held for them will conclude. Others would have it lengthened so they would be able to stuff even more activities and accomplishments into it.

My way would be for you to live your life and view your life second by second. This is why I created an internal "clock of life" within you—your heart. This precious organ of life pumps life-sustaining blood to your body. However, it also serves as a timer of life. Each heartbeat is one that will never be regained. Why do you not walk in awareness of this truth? I do not wish for you to cling to the seconds or to be anxious about their passage. I want you to see them as a treasure—an investment—as a communion with Me.

If I had wanted you to measure your days in hours, I would have designed your heart to beat once each hour. If 1 had wanted your life to be measured in minutes, I would have designed a rhythm of beats that are 60 seconds apart. Instead, I ordained one heartbeat to be, on the average, one second before another and one second after the previous one. Gather up your days by the seconds that I give to you, little one. Allow Me to reign over each of those seconds. Then, watch Me change them into a blessed lifetime, and into a glorious eternity.

SWALLOWS AND SWIFTS

Swallows and swifts are birds that I've designed for graceful flight. Like streamlined precision experts, they course through the skies in unending dives and curves. How restless they seem to be to the observer. Yet, they are at peace.

These precious creations are never content with stillness and they are never concerned with barriers. Their patterns in the skies joyously continue—darting swiftly in and out and up and down. Creating the artwork of silent patterns in the sky, they fly in praise of their being. Tiny crevices become a home in which they can find rest, or nest their young.

Why do swifts and swallows do what they do? They do so because it brings them joy to practice the perfection in which I have created within them. Is it burdensome work and boredom to fly in endless patterns? No! To do what one has been created to do is the highest of all joys!

Take a lesson from the swifts and swallows, little one. Very little variation fills their days, and yet, they remain joyful as they do so well what I have enabled them to do.

What makes you joyful? Your behavior declares that variety and striving for greater activity and accomplishment pleases you. Without these things, boredom overtakes you. Look into yourself. For what have you been created? You have been created for relationship, not for isolation. You have been created to reach high and to grow toward Me. But these things are never to be endless, joyless patterns. If you are engaged in living and not merely in observing life, you will want to busy yourself building things that will last. That is what your spirit speaks into your soul.

Notice what happens when your joy leaves you. Why have you stopped building and stretching? Why have you given yourself to the darting and circling about that was designed for the swallows and swifts? Your journey is to be ever upward, not horizontally, circular, or downward. Look deeply into your feeling of discontent, and you will see that you have ceased doing that for which you have been created—building upward vision, and adding glory to eternity.

So, come out of your endless patterns. Come out of your ways of darting about with little rest or joy. Live out of *your* own individual design and purpose rather than taking on the course of any of My other created children.

Come and light upon the palm of My hand. Fold in your wings and rest. Learn of Me. This is where your joy will be found. Give yourself into My keeping, and I shall show you how to live out your design. Then, both in the learning and in the practice of it we two shall know great joy.

BEACH TREASURES

Absorb the beauty of My ocean. Do not stand back from it. Don't only turn your eyes and ears to the pounding surf, but turn your heart to it, as well. Celebrate the love I have put into My seas and oceans. Dig your toes into the soft sand. Soothe your feet in the cool, salty water. Listen to the cry of the seabirds.

Come, walk along the beach with Me. Let us hunt for treasures together. Look past the signs of waste and trash from humans who have callous indifference to My beaches. Overlook the glass shards, the tar from spilled oil, the paper and plastic and metal pieces that serve no further function. Focus on the gifts—not on the garbage! See the tiny shells scattered about—tiny pink and beige treasures. But remember, if you look too quickly, you will miss them. They are not present in great abundance, for if they were, they would lose the certain quality of their preciousness. That which is truly precious is rare.

Watch the water's edge. Watch where the waves have exhausted themselves in their climb to the shore and watch where they now retreat. At the edge you will see the small shells as they toss about and settle briefly. Be quick in capturing one of these treasures. In the blink of an eye it may be gone. A new wave may claim it and pull it back into the sea.

Do not ignore the plain, white shells either. Turn them over to find the color I have painted on their sunward sides, which are now inverted in the sand. Dig out those half-buried shells, and do not discard the chipped or broken treasures. They still belong to Me. And even in their brokenness, I cherish them.

There is a vast beach of treasure in My human creation, little one. People are much like these tiny, fragile shells that are being tossed onto the beaches of life by powerful tides of living.

Many land on high, safe ground, while others lie in precariously unsure places. These latter ones lie ready to be dragged backward into the depths, but My movement is always forward. Reach down and pick them up. Move these little ones to higher ground.

Some lie upside down. They are inverted causing their colors to remain unseen. Such shells are often overlooked by people. They are considered to be too plain and ordinary—not interesting or valuable. Turn them over lovingly and rinse away the things that hide their beauty. In the same way, lovingly and gently dig out My partially buried children, those who are stuck and being overcome and swallowed by the beachhead.

Get them up and out of that which "buries them alive." The "sand" that suffocates them is bitterness, imprisoned memories, anger, and destructive patterns and habits in themselves or others.

These little ones cannot find their own way. They need the touch of one who is willing to get grit and sand on his or her hands and under their fingernails. Sometimes the "digging out" requires an investment of time. So, invest your time where I tell you to invest it. Do not spend your time where I have not told you to work.

In all your treasure hunting, never, ever discard the imperfect and broken children of life. Each one has a place and a purpose.

The jagged, sharp edge on a shell can become a cutting tool in the hands of a craftsman. Give Me these little ones, which the world would discard through abortion or by abandonment, and I, the Master Craftsman, will make beautiful etchings on the world with them.

LOCKED DOORS

Doors, once locked, can provide a sense of joy and safety, or they can be a source of frustration and deprivation. Why do you lock doors, little one? Most would say they do so to keep all threats outside.

Do you not also lock doors to keep things in? If you had a precious treasure that you wanted to keep secure, a locked door would be a wall of protection against a thief. But, in maintaining its safety, you might not be able to celebrate or admire it beyond the confines of the room in which it is kept.

If a swarm of flies were to try and invade your dwelling, it would be good to close and lock the door. In so doing, you would both keep them out, and protect your home and loved ones from any diseases they might be carrying. If the flies, however, were able to swarm through an open door, would you not leave the door fully open until you were able to drive them out? It would be a foolish thing to lock them in, only to chase them one by one and kill them individually.

Consider the "doors" in My human creation. There are doors to the mind, the spirit, and the body. Do you not see them?

Undeserved pain and suffering can open doors in many areas of your life. The experience of rejection, for example, causes an imprint of pain to be left upon one's body, soul, and spirit. If you were so wounded, would you not wish to close yourself off from future injury? However, not expelling the pain and its companions first would mean that the pain of rejection would stay locked within you. The "flies" of it would buzz about, bringing destruction and disease.

If you observed the pain of rejection in others and sought to avoid it by locking the doors to your own soul, what would the result be? In your effort to protect the treasure within you from being taken, you would also lock away that which is precious from the world.

Little ones, seek Me. I am the One who expels all manifestations of personal pain from your life. I am your Deliverer and the Healer.

Do not seek to slay the flies individually, by your own efforts. Instead, allow Me to open wide the door by which they came, and then I shall drive them away. Let Me breathe in the freshness of My Spirit to clean and refurbish the rooms of your innermost being.

If you fear the attacker and would seek protection, allow Me to stand guard at the entryway. Allow Me to hold the keys and the authority to use them at will. Often, I will lock doors against the attacks of the enemy. Sometimes I open the door when there is safety, so that the brilliance of the treasure within can be seen and enjoyed by many. Then, on rare occasions, when I have planted a precious seed to grow within you, I will seal off the place for a while, so it will have the time and the protection to grow into full treasure.

Give Me the keys to your doors. I am your Guardian, and I am your Sustainer-Refiner. Let Me do the deep work of airing out the "rooms of infestation" within you. Allow Me the honor of exposing your gifts to the world which is so desperately in need of them.

Put aside all fear, and give Me the keys. There is no better watchman than Me.

SILVER GOBLETS

How excellent is the work of My hands! Did you not know that I am a Craftsman of many precious things? Surely you have seen My excellent work in the children I have created by My own hands. Truly, they are all precious, for each one bears the stamp of the authenticity of the Master Craftsman. Each one is as a pure silver goblet.

Why a goblet, not a plate? A goblet is a thing of great beauty, and it requires more skill to create it than it does to create a plate. A plate lays low, while a goblet stands up high above the plate. The shapes of plates may vary somewhat, but the shapes of goblets vary a great deal. As a goblet stands upon a table, it can easily admire the etchings and carvings engraved around it. The lowly plate, on the other hand, must be lifted up, empty, in one's hands in order to show forth its beauty.

A plate may be a "servant" that is met by a spoon or fork, but seldom is it lifted up to the lips directly to distribute its gifts. It is not so with the goblet, however. The goblet was created for a more direct form of "servanthood," to carry the treasure of its contents directly to one's lips. Unlike the plate, it needs no other utensil to assist it. While the hand may reach into the plate to acquire its treasures, the hand does not reach into the goblet potentially soiling its contents to obtain its gift.

I created all My children, little one, to stand tall and bear My gifts directly to those in need. They are to be containers and reservoirs of My love and glory, but not in a passive way. Instead, they are to be direct carriers of My essence to others. They are not to be tainted by the touch of unclean hands. They themselves are to be lifted up to thirsty lips in order to bring forth holy contents.

The stem of a goblet is designed to invite one's hand to grasp it with ease. Looking somewhat delicate, it has both strength and balance.

Which is more immediately vital to maintain life? Is it liquid or solid food? Of course it is liquids. Without fluid, the body will die within days. True, a plate may hold a bit of liquid, but it does so to its disadvantage, for liquids are so easily spilled from a plate. The form of a goblet, however, invites fullness. It is like an open belly that is waiting to be filled with nectar.

An unused, empty goblet is frustrated by its emptiness, while a full one, as it touches one's lips, is fulfilled. Do you see this; do you understand this comparison? How I want My children to be filled with new wine and with living water. I delight to see them spilling over. I delight to see them delivering their gifts to the spiritually parched and dying.

My hand lifts them up like goblets which I've designed for My purposes for I own each goblet, and each is engraved with My name and polished by My hand. But there are also goblets with unseen stamps that are hidden behind a veil of tarnish.

There are goblets that are dull and dark; demonstrating no brilliant shine. Yes, these are the ones who have been handled by the unclean hands of the world and by My enemy. Tragically they bear the evidence of this handling. They have refused to acknowledge the Craftsman's stamp under the tarnish, not allowing the stamp to be made visible. They have refused My polishing hand. They are both self-possessed and world-possessed.

Unlike an actual goblet that sits passively by, awaiting the touch of any hand that would embrace it, many of My children have used their freedom of choice to deface the mark I have given to them in love, which claims them as My own.

Unlike an actual goblet of silver that passively awaits the polishing cloth, My children have the choice to refuse or seek such cleaning. Each touch of the world upon My children leaves a residue of destruction. This residue interacts with the putrid breath of the prince of this world to form a killing tarnish. At first, this only covers the shine, but eventually it pits and erodes the precious silver out of which the goblet was crafted.

Who would accept such a destructive touch? Sadly, many seem to be eager to receive it. They have been told that to truly exercise their freedom to choose, they must choose freedom from My ownership and from My touch. This deception is loudly heard. Often, it is heard even within the walls of those places that are called sanctuaries of My Word and My Spirit.

These precious goblets are told about the way they were created and crafted, but they are left believing that they are now free to choose a life without My touch. They are given over to the world's handling—into the fingers of My enemy. They erroneously see this as freedom.

Can a darkened, pitted goblet ever be reclaimed? Can it be used as a vessel? For common and dishonored use it might be quite sufficient, but who would lift up such a vessel at a banquet of honor? Who would pour the finest of wines into it or celebrate a great victory with a dented tarnished vessel? Who would toast the bride and groom with such a goblet?

And yet, these damaged goblets can be reclaimed. Once warmed in the fire of reclamation, the dents and the bruises will be tapped out by the Master. That glow, formerly hidden by unholy residue, can be recovered by the hand of the Polisher and by the substance and the cloth used for the polishing. What has been bent can be straightened, so it again may stand tall and majestic.

Do I reject the tarnished, damaged "goblets"? No, because I see in each one the substance of his or her creation. I see the love which formed them. Indeed, I ever remember it. Yet, I would lovingly desire for each one to be subjected to the heat of fire again and to submit to the pressure of the tongs and hammer. I would remove the tarnish and the darkness with a polish of My own making. My polish is made of the "oil of repentance," mixed with the abrasion of consequences and infused with the redeeming lifeblood of My love. Whenever a darkened or damaged child cries out for reclamation I take great delight in applying the formula of My restoration.

It is my joy to take a polishing cloth in My hand in order to restore them to glory and brilliance. I would delight to rinse each one under My stream of living water. With droplets of new life clinging to the surface, I would withdraw these "goblets" from the living water. I would sing with joy and weep with tenderness at the restored glory of My original labor and handiwork.

So, cry out, dark little goblets of silver! You have forgotten your substance. You have forgotten your Craftsman. You have forgotten your true function.

Cry out to be restored, and I shall be quick to make it happen. You have been too long accustomed to the darkness and the defacing touch. You have been too long jealous of those I have polished to the brightest levels of shining. You have cried out in envy against My goblets of high and holy use.

Why do you despise those who serve as a sign to you of your own holy origin and calling? You are deceived. It is this holiness that you have decried to which you have been called. So, see the shining ones with new eyes. See them with eyes of longing, hope, and promise. Remember, it was for such a purpose that you were created. For such honor and freedom you were formed by My hand.

Call out for My hand now, little goblets! I have need of you to be richly filled, to be brilliant in your luster. Reject the lies of the enemy concerning My glory in you. Hear Me, for it is not too late to be reclaimed and reformed, but do not wait! The time is short. The thirsty are waiting. I need you to be filled, to stand, to shine, and to carry My love to them. My loving hand is ready to reclaim you!

THE MATCH

So, you wish to ignite a fire within you, little one? You have asked for a fire of passion for My Word and My presence to burn within you. You have asked for an endowment of the fire of love and compassion toward others to flame up in your heart. It is well that you request these things. And yet, I wonder if you know what you are asking for. Do you know the price of such a fire?

How does one begin a fire in a hearth? Besides the kindling, one would require a match or perhaps a flint. In either case, that which would offer itself up to ignite the spark offers itself up for pain and loss. To yield oneself up to striking, to feel the pain of the blow and the friction against a hard and unrelenting surface is a sacrificial act.

Is a flame in the soul or spirit birthed in a different way? In some ways no, but yet in many ways, yes. To begin a fire, the match must be held tightly. To begin a flame within you, I must hold you firmly in My grasp. If I did not hold you tightly, you would give way to the rubbing and nothing would be accomplished except an abrasion. If I would hold you too rigidly, or strike too hard, you would break even as a wooden match would break.

Be careful regarding who you allow to take hold of you. I alone must possess you. No other person of flesh or spirit is to have control of your course. I alone will always hold you in firm tenderness. I alone know the proper pressure to apply to the striking surface. I alone know the correct angle to contact the source of friction, out of which the flame will arise.

Look now to the surface of the match. What quality of the match makes the spark possible? Is it not the chemical mix that is created and placed upon the match which provides the potential for a flame? If you are to bring forth both light and heat, you must be specifically created with the mix of soul and spirit that would yield itself to the task. Throughout your life, I have always been and always will be about the business of creating this wonderful mix of experience, learning, understanding, emotion, and priority. When all these things are in perfect placement and quantity, the match will be nearly ready.

Now look to your surrounding conditions and environment. These speak to you of external factors. The circumstances and environment impacting the wooden match might take the form of surrounding moisture or too strong a prevailing wind. For instance, if the match were to encounter moisture, a strike would yield only disintegration without a fire. If the match were struck in an unrestrained wind, the flame would die at birth.

Allow Me to arrange not only your internal conditions, but your external ones as well. I can order all things, so that which you long to bring forth, will do so with effective and lasting results.

Finally, look to the striking surface and to the process of striking the match itself. If the striking surface on a matchbox is worn down too smoothly, the match will never light, no matter how often it is struck. Likewise, the surface of the match should not be too coarse. If you would try to strike a match upon a brick wall, you would see the match fall apart, because the resistance would be too harsh—too great for successful lighting.

The "striking surfaces" within the lives of My children come in many forms. It may be a trial concerning his or her reputation. It could come in the form of a loss. Similarly, it may involve a great decision or temptation.

Whatever the case, I know the exact thing that will be needed to bring forth your fire. It shall not be so mild that there is no impact, except to wear you down gradually. Nor shall it be so harsh that you would be destroyed by it. In My wisdom, it shall be the exact level of discomfort that is required to ignite the mix of your soul and spirit into a joyous blaze.

TRAINING

Little one, the life of joy and safety and effectiveness is the life of discipline. It is a life of constant learning and practice. Little things provide the subjects of learning and teaching at the beginning. The basics of the journey must always come first, however.

Before a building can be constructed, its foundation must be laid, and before a child learns to come at the call of his parents, he must first learn the sound of his own name.

The life of faith is learned step by step and teaching by teaching. The beginning exercises will seem so clumsy, because there is much stumbling involved in learning to walk before a child can learn to run. This learning is accomplished through the scraped knees and from the bruised noses as a result of falls suffered by the unsteady and inexperienced. In these ways the child in training learns the skills of balance.

It is only through first listening to a loud voice calling out instructions during training that the guide dog learns to respond instantly to a whispered command or a tug on its harness.

Recognition of the voice of the trainer comes first. Then comes the taking of the first steps, followed by responding to directions with obedience. These are the essential elements of training.

Would you prefer not to take this course? What is the cost? Without training, one is unprepared for the journey, its tasks, and its challenges. How could a soldier learn to handle his weapons without training? How could he achieve the full level of preparedness without exercise? What general would call new, untrained recruits onto the battlefield? He would not do so, because he would know they would all be destroyed in such a case.

No one likes the rigors of hard training. At first, the muscles ache and cry out. The lungs heave and the heart pounds with fatigue. The mind seeks diversion and relaxation. The feet would like to run away, but let the training continue and observe what happens.

The body becomes strong and resilient. The mind becomes focused and knowledgeable. The heart turns toward obedience. The ears and the eyes discern.

Do not resist My training program. Come and learn your name. Recognize My voice calling you. Learn to yield to My instruction and to My timetable. Study both your weaponry and the enemy's. I want you to be strong. I want you to be prepared and effective. I want you to be safe.

All these things come from knowing Me and from spending time in My training camp. Do not worry. All your nourishment and equipment are there, and each is marked with your name. Simply come, step forward and commit yourself to the training. My finger points at you. My word says, "I want you!" I want you not as a puppet or a mercenary. I want you as a holy warrior who wears the insignia of My Kingdom.

Come and let the training begin now.

DIGGINGS

What mysteries lie buried underground, little one? Are you curious to find out? Is there not enough to explore on the surface of the earth that you should begin digging in the soil to find more?

My children have an innate desire for more knowledge, more excitement, and more possession. Therefore, they dig. But do you understand what you have found when you hold in your hand what has been disclosed?

For some of My children the thrill is in the finding. They are little concerned about understanding what they find. Others seek the joy of ownership—of trophy and prize to possess. Still others care only for what the treasure can bring to them on the market. None of these truly understands the significance of the digging, however.

To dig and to expose what has been hidden is to seek after foundations. What came before is the foundation of what currently is. This is so important to understand. If what is built on top seems shaky or skewed, check to see what lies underneath.

This applies not only to archeology, but also to present-day life. To discover why the great governments and civilizations of the past have fallen, dig out their ruins, for they will teach you. A culture that is too heavy in gold, a culture that is built upon idolatry, a culture which embraces the shedding of innocent blood and the cause of wickedness will show these weaknesses and failings in its foundations. The remains left behind will reveal these things.

If a present-day family stands in ruins, dig under its broken fragments to discover what its foundation consists of and was built upon. In so doing, you will likely find shards of unforgiveness, overindulgence, selfishness, bitterness, weakness, and unholiness.

You will discover that it was not just the existence of these things in the present day that caused the ruin, buried deep underneath you will find things in and under the foundation that have led to the present condition.

If this is not understood, one ruin will become the site of still another ruin, because the foundation remains the same. The circumstances and the persons may vary, but the eventual ruin will be assured.

So, dig down first before you attempt to build any structure. Dig under your brokenness and your pain. See where the cisterns of love have become cracked and were never filled. See where inferior building materials were used. Such inferior materials may take the form of self-sufficiency, deception, and closed minds. Once you discover these things, don't just study them, and then shake your head and walk away from them. Begin the work of replacing that which has become rotten with that which is strong and good.

Allow Me, by My Spirit, to guide, direct, and contract this work. Permit Me to go into the ancient ruins with you to instruct you in the examination. If you would go into the ruins and begin madly tearing things up and pulling things apart, you would destroy the potential for learning from the broken things. To uncover only partially that which lies buried, only to surmise what else there might be, yields only deception and partial truth.

Some things that are buried in the ruins will be glued together to restore their former function and beauty that had been lost to time and pressure. Other things were never meant to be repaired—only discarded. These are the reasons why I, alone, must direct the dig. Only I know what each piece represents and where each belongs. Only I know the past, the present, and the future. Do not attempt to do this work alone, but do not neglect to do it.

Within you there is a buried treasure among the broken shards of pain. I can build a treasure house for that which is good and valuable. I alone can haul away the refuse.

That which stands upon a foundation of the past is only as secure as the foundation itself. If I am not the support structure underneath, there will be perpetual weakness and the danger of ruin. Stop wasting your time and your energy, trying to shore up that which needs to be brought down by My hand. Give Me the shovel and the pickax. Give Me your insufficient blueprint. Allow Me to show you the mysteries of the digging. Together we shall uncover the truth, and together we shall evaluate, clean, and polish. Together we shall build a new foundation that will stand throughout eternity, a foundation that will support all which I direct you to build upon it.

Come! Roll up your sleeves! Prepare to be exposed to the darkness and the dirt underneath your collapsed dreams and efforts. I shall provide the light, and we shall work side by side. Together we shall find the pieces you need to bring understanding to you. Unlike the puppy, who digs for the joy of uprooting, we shall dig for the joy of rebuilding.

POLLEN

What are these invisible messengers of new life that are blowing through the air? They are picked up by the bodies of bees and carried from flower to flower. It is pollen, and how precious pollen is to a blossom. As it is carried by the wind or by a bee, it brings the promise of fruit. It also brings the hope of continued new life for the plant.

The plant rejoices in the pollen, but other creatures in My creation do not. However, to the bee it is an inconvenience that must be accepted along with the harvest of nectar. The nectar of the flower is the treasure for the bee not the pollen.

Similarly, the treasure for My human creation is the flower itself, the honey that comes from the flower nectar, and the fruit from the flower. To many people, the pollen is only a source of irritation to their nose, eye, and throat. Some try to reject its presence by a sneeze, a tear, or a blow. Some cry out against it by medicating themselves against its effects.

But what if life was free of pollen? There would be no flower, no fruit, no honey. What seems to be an unnecessary annoyance is truly vital. Many beautiful, sweet, and nourishing blessings come from it.

What in your life is like pollen, little one? Is it daily work at your job? Is it a person who constantly annoys you? Is it a responsibility that weighs heavily upon you? What is it that you cry out against in irritation? What is it that you would reject or want to cast away? What is it that you "medicate" away by diversion or entertainment?

What seems to be an annoyance in your life is very often vital to your growth and maturation. What seems to be too great an irritation may well be the beginning of new life. Do not be too quick to decry any form of "pollen" in your life. With these things new learning and new growth come, and they will bring forth new blossoms in your life. The blossoms will bring forth sweet fruit.

Therefore, learn to appreciate the pollen in your life. Learn even to praise Me for it. It may not be pleasing. It may not be comfortable or convenient either. However, as you look to Me for wisdom and direction in these things, you shall learn to rejoice in them. I understand that your flesh may reject My "pollen" in your life. But learn to embrace it in your spirit.

Even as the flower draws the transported pollen into its innermost parts, so, also, you need to take the message My pollen provides into the innermost parts of your spirit. Here is where the new seeds will form. Here is the place from which new life will spring. Do not sneeze at My pollen in an effort to rid yourself of it; simply, breathe deeply of its treasure. Bring forth new life, and grow!

BONFIRES

The night air is filled with the smoke of many bonfires in celebration of a holiday. There is dancing and singing in the land. A holy remembrance arises in the glow of the fires. It speaks of the righteousness of Abba and of the love bestowed in forgiveness. This is a holy bonfire, and its smoke is pleasing.

Yet, at the same time, some fires are burning that are not holy. These are fires of flesh and entertainment—fires of vain frolic and overindulgence. These are not pleasing to Me. There is no holy meaning in these fires, for they are only a vain show.

Holy fires can be mingled with unholy ones. Their smoke rises together, first in separate columns and then mingled together in a single blanket that covers the land.

In times of evil, bonfires will burn. Some burn to destroy holy writings and moral teachings. Others burn as an incinerator for the bodies of the dead—those who are diseased, in want, killed in battle, or sacrificed to unrighteousness. Some raise up flames to destroy the holy witness by destroying those who bring it to the people.

Be watchful, little one, for if the first fires—the holy ones—fail to be lit or to be kept burning, or if those who have been assigned to light them turn aside to celebrate and forget the reason for their burning, they shall become the sites of unholy fires.

Remember the sweet scent of incense? A small ember can fill the whole house with its essence. Likewise, a seared piece of healthy steak that is left to char in the flame of a grill can also fill the house with a welcome scent. But if the flesh is rotten or diseased, and if it is allowed to smolder continually, the stench of it not only fills the house, but all other surrounding dwellings, as well.

Keep your heart pure. Keep your vision clear and make sure your memory of godly things is always present. Should you fail to do so, very quickly a stench will arise.

Do not build or join in with the pagan fires of idolatry. These bonfires in the dark of night invite unholy rituals and sacrifices from the very pit of hell.

Always choose purity. Choose to offer up holy sacrifices and celebrations. Let these holy bonfires burn brightly within you. Let them draw others to their warmth and to their sweet fragrance. Let them draw My children to *Me*. In holy fire, burn sweetly!

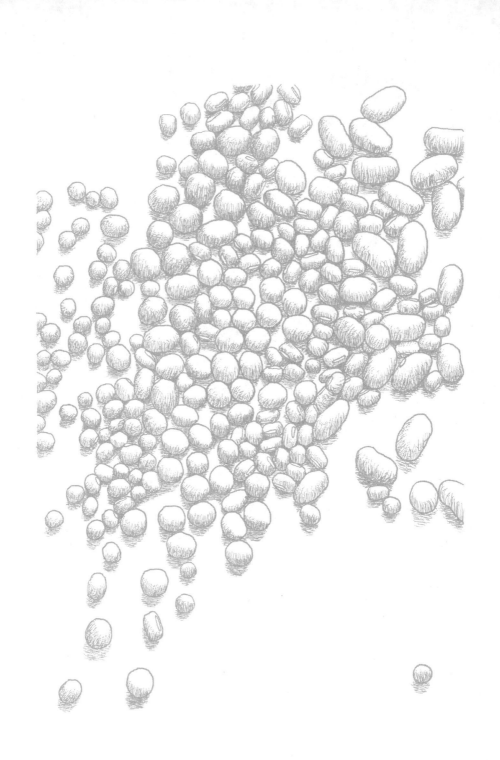

SORTING

Reach up, little one. The Kingdom of God is increasingly near you. Your words are to proclaim it. Your activities are to give witness to it. Even your very thoughts should always radiate its truths.

Renew your mind. Subdue your emotions so that they come under My authority. Choose to think about the truths of My Word. In the same way that you sort dried beans before you cook and eat them, sort your thoughts, because they will become food for your spirit.

Some thoughts will be "sickened" in the natural, as they flow through eroded flesh. Some will flow into your mind as planted inspirations from My enemy. These thoughts are actually "pebbles" posing as "beans."

Every thought that comes to you must be continually washed in living water in order to remove the debris and to disclose their true nature and character. The dust of the earth must be washed away. As your thoughts are washed, the stones that are posing as beans will be clearly evidenced.

It takes time to sort and inspect the dried beans. Sometimes this sorting may be a bother to you and an encumbrance upon your time. Just remember that it takes far greater time and focus to sort human thoughts than it takes to sort beans. Scientists of the mind say that this is impossible, because they say that the mind receives passively—a victim of influence from exterior and interior forces that are subject to the words that come to it. This is not so. The renewed mind has the ability to differentiate between and to discern thoughts as they form. It has the ability to then turn them away before they are absorbed into the mind's processing.

Seek this mental discipline. Seek the anointing of your mind, which will enable you to function as one who has been renewed. Your emotions rise out of your thoughts and perceptions. In renewing your mind, you subject your emotions to My authority, as well.

The unholy, undisciplined mind harbors and creates unholy, undisciplined emotional responses. These neither serve Me nor My Kingdom. Embrace this truth and walk in it. Teach it to others. Pray My anointing upon others, so that they, too, can draw near to Me and to My shalom. Do this so that shalom might come to the Body of Messiah, where there is now disorder and strife. Sort out the stones from the food, and then enjoy the great banquet in which I have provided for you.

THE BLIND LEADING THE BLIND

Can you feel the beginning wind upon your face, little one? So many have turned their backs to it, hoping to ignore it as it were in their imaginations. Listen! Do you hear the distant thunder? So many have been too busy with their loud music of merrymaking to notice it. What about the lightning and the dark clouds?

Have your eyes been turned toward them? So many of My children are blind to their approach, because the world has placed scales across their eyes, blinding scales that I would remove, if they would only ask. Too many enjoy the distorted view through the scales. How then shall they protect themselves and how can they prepare for that which is coming in the wind? These are careless, uncommitted children, who seek to be led blindly, by others who are blind as well. They seek the wisdom of blind men. What folly this is! How can one who is sightless know the correct path to follow when there are so many from which to choose? Whether in a place of total darkness or bright sunlight their perception is always the same. Blind guides often feel confident in their application of logic and their intellect. They say that they know the way, for they have thought it through and used their reason to find it. Others have blindly submitted their journey to the direction of unholy spirit guides who are inspired by My enemy. They mistakenly believe them to be benevolent bringers of divine truth.

Consider the cost of such deception. A blind man may reason himself to be on safe ground because he can hear the pounding surf of the distant ocean. "Surely, it is far from me!" he reasons. And yet he may be quickly approaching the edge of a great cliff high above the sea.

"Come and follow me!" he shouts to his blind companions. "I know the way; we are safe on this course!" What folly it is to be so close to death while still holding on to the arrogance of false knowledge! How hideous it is to lead others to death, as well.

When the blind leader plummets from the cliff, will not the others hear his cries of distress and panic? Will they then turn to retreat? This is unlikely. Those who follow behind him will have found the thought of hazard to be insulting to their own knowledge and capabilities. They will have found it too frightening to consider the possibilities.

These followers have heard the voice of their blind leader, and they have believed his lies. They have believed the deception that he truly has sight and that he will always warn them of danger. They believe he surely will always lead them in truth! They have closed off their ears to other voices, especially to My prompting. They deny any reality other than the false reality through which they have been led along in comfort.

Little one, to ever close off your ears and your heart to My word would mean that error would surely come to you. With it collective blindness, worldliness, and even death will come. My child, your perceptions of mind and flesh that were created in your own understanding without the wisdom of My Spirit are in error! You cannot read My word without holy, spiritual eyes. You cannot hear My words without holy, spiritual ears. You cannot walk in truth when you are walking in flesh alone, because the flesh has been corrupted by My enemy!

To be led in safety and in truth, I must lead you. In order for Me to truly lead, you must surrender to My wisdom and authority. Call out My name and I shall come to you. Just call it! Too many use My name and know My name, but they do not honor My name by living in submission to it. Many use My name to blame me for the pain that they have caused themselves. Call to Me as one who is willing to follow the authority of the One who possesses the name.

I am a purveyor of vision. I long for My children to see those things to which the world is blind. In the darkness, I shall hold on to your hand. In the bright light, I shall allow you the pleasure of freedom to follow My call. Stop all further advances in any direction, if you are hearkening to any voice other than Mine. Put aside the arrogance that comes from following your own course.

Too many are rapidly approaching the great cliff, because they are being led blindly along in the company of others who are blind. Choose to walk in the company of the sighted, in the company of those who honor Me and follow My lead. Then you shall not only walk in safety, but also in joy, peace, and deep fulfillment.

CHOOSING DISOBEDIENCE

Little one, you are bothered by the question of the lost. What should I tell you to put your heart at ease? Scripture is very clear about these things. I mourn and grieve the eternal loss of My own created children. And yet, what else can I do? Can I change the eternal law of atonement? Should I violate My own Word? Am I not just? Have I not extended My hand to save time and time again? Either I am just, or I am not at all.

My children who choose to live in defiance and rebellion— what should I do for them that I have not already done? I have clearly given My Word and My grace. I have provided a lifetime of opportunities and faithful witnesses who have spoken of My truth. My Spirit constantly moves over the face of the earth, bringing inspirations of My truth to those who would receive them.

When a choice to defy Me is made, whose fault is it? Is it a generational curse that comes through the family line? Is it the sins of one's parents? Is it the painful circumstances of one's life that are to blame? Am I so hard and so blind that My grace does not continually cover these things?

If someone is in bondage to spiritual darkness, is he left helpless? NO! I have provided for them and I have waited with love for the rebellious ones to return. I have provided pathways before them on which to journey back to Me.

Such people deceive themselves and often others, however, by the sweet rationale and explanations that flow from their lips. I send to them trials to awaken them to truth, so they will understand the spiritual dangers they face. In the final analysis, though, the choice is always theirs, and I am always there to assist them in making the choice to receive My wholeness.

They choose, but they choose disobedience. They choose to believe they will be the great exception to My divine law. They think, "Surely God's arms are big enough to embrace me as I am." Yes, I am big enough to embrace them, but I am too righteous to pull sin into My own bosom. My Word is clear about this. Why, then, do they not listen? Do they think I am fiction, just some creation of human fantasy?

My mercy truly endures forever, but so, also, does My righteousness endure. My human creation no longer fears My righteousness. It no longer believes it to be reality. My holiness is the measuring rod against which no man can stand. The Messiah will stand in the place of anyone who would turn from sin and embrace His righteousness. So, embrace it! Embrace it, and do not fill your head with only knowledge of it! Yield your sinful nature to the embrace of holiness. Cling to Me, and die to your bent toward sinning. I will enable you to do this vital thing. You must only choose, cry out, and embrace. I wait, and I cry out to you, weeping.

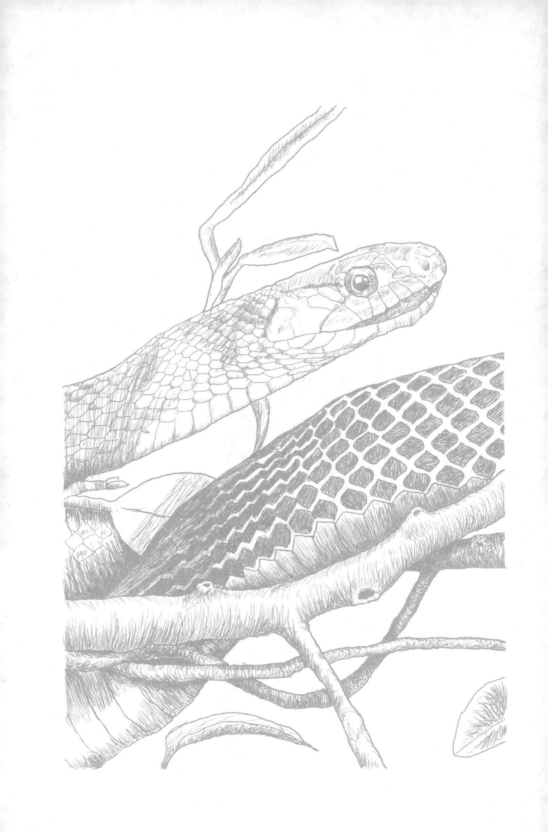

FEAR AND COBRAS

Little one, listen to the sound of fear in the hearts of men. What is its tone? What is its timbre and its quality? Out of the heart that fears comes the cacophony of lies, anger, self-protection, and control. When you hear these sounds, be sure to examine their origin. What is the source of the fear? Is it fear that arises from the manipulation created by My enemy?

This tactic by the deceiver is meant to immobilize and cripple My children. His words ring out, "Danger! Behold, this is not good and true. You are unsafe. Things of God will harm and disappoint you. They will confine you and will remove your freedom to enjoy life." These lies cause My children to seek false shelter in that which is both familiar and unsafe, because they are ignorant of the ploy. They are caused to flee from Me because of these lies, when they should be bowing in prayer. Is My hand so short that I would not protect those who would seek My guidance and My care?

Watch for the effect of all words of fear. Look to the fruit of fear—its bitter offspring born out of deception. You will see manipulation. You will see attacks of anxiety. You will see people hiding behind past events and understandings. You will see the spirit of the persecutor arising with his stinging whip of cruel words directed toward others.

The way of My Kingdom is expansion. In the presence of fear, you will see constriction. What was once easy and confident becomes stressed and uncertain. What was surely known is questioned and doubted. In fear's presence, My Word will be lost or abandoned, and even bent at times. In all ways, the shalom is lost to those who are given over to the deceiver's grasp of fear.

But what of holy fear? What are its sounds? In holy fear, which is true reverence of Me, you will find the sounds of weeping and humility. Holy fear brings forth children of surrender and obedience—children of repentance and the grace of forgiveness. There will be no lies or slander there. Truth will stand untainted by the charges of the Pharisees.

There will be an opening up of human hearts to godly touches and encounters in order to purify My children. The appetite for a deeper knowing of Me shall break forth, and people shall be fed. There shall be sounds of holy laughter and rejoicing. There shall be sounds of holy worship of the Most High, worship in spirit and in truth and in freedom.

Which kind of fear runs rampant on the face of the earth? Which is embraced and which is rebuked? When unholy fear reigns, godly fear will be mocked and slandered. Those who walk in holy fear will be scorned because he who stokes the fires of unholy fear mocks and hates Me.

What should be My children's response to unholy fear? It should be met with a well-placed wall of faith. Fear, which arises in the unholy claims that surrender and faith, are foolish, even dangerous. It calls out to stay with those things in which are safe and familiar, even if those very things would bring death to body, mind, or spirit. As the spit venom of a cobra blinds, so does fear blind

My children. As the injected venom of the viper paralyzes and kills the body, so does unholy fear in My Body of believers. Whether spewed forth from the mouth in seemingly endless droplets of gossip or by bitter lies injected directly into the members of the body, death is equally assured.

Behold, the cobra can be charmed for a time, but is it any less deadly as a result? You can manipulate unholy fear for a time, but know that it can unloose its deadly venom at any moment. There are those of My misguided children who manipulate fear by using it to fascinate others or to bring personal or financial gain. Using the power of fear, they gain attention through creating a mesmerizing "side show" or while deceiving others and themselves with the lie that things are truly under control. Many times those who would be confident of their "cobras in the basket" have fallen victim to their sudden, unexpected strike!

Put down unholy fear, My children. Seal its enticing, sweet sounds from your hearts and your spirits. Remember to do this when they call you to embrace them for any reason.

Always dress yourself in holy fear. In My perfect love, you shall deflect the cobra's strike and venom. Your words and your actions will ring with truth and with peace. Division shall not enter your heart, as unity with My Spirit will draw the fragments of knowledge and understanding together. Faith shall be the filler and the cement that will create the mosaic of holy wisdom.

Do not turn your back on the cobra. It can as easily destroy your life from behind as it can from the front. Cover your eyes with the lens of My Word and My truth. Pick up the sword of faith, and lop off the head of this cobra of fear. Do not allow it to slither away to strike again in another time and place.

Unholy fear has always risen up to destroy My faithful and to destroy My Word in them. Holy fear has always ascended to the heights above its range. Be about the business of learning holy fear. Come to know Me, not just to know about Me. Come to Me in holy fear and in trembling first. Then come in confidence and in joy. Your fear and trembling will equip you to defeat My enemy. In confidence and in joy, we two shall commune together.

Behold, the cobras are multiplying at an increasing rate. Come to Me quickly, that your faith might be multiplied. Hesitate in order to be fascinated by the cobras' movements, or toy with them or turn your back toward them and ignore their presence, and your faith may perish in an unexpected attack. In that perilous moment, you shall be in danger of being transformed. In the bite of fear, with the venom circulating throughout your being, even you could be transformed into a cobra! Take heed.

THORNS

How have you experienced thorns, little one? Have they been the price you've had to pay for gathering roses? Have they been a surprise of pain to your bare feet? Do they say to you, "Do not touch"? Why are there thorns in the world? What was I thinking of when I formed them? Were they the result of a fallen, broken creation that came about after sin entered My perfect world?

Thorns present contrasts into My creation, do they not? How can a beautiful rose be endowed with such a hazard? How can ripe, juicy berries beg to be picked, and yet cost you dearly for touching them?

Thorns have come forth to speak of challenged vulnerability. While they convey the suggestion of self-protection for their bearer, they become the declaration of cost to those who would be vulnerable to their touch. In the beginning, My human children were without hazard. They only needed to feel vulnerable to My love—never to pain. The advent of sin changed that reality.

Many of My wounded children bear in their bodies, minds, and spirits the wounds of embedded thorns. They have come to them by the actions and words of the careless and the self-protected—those with evil intent and those who have acted in ignorance. Some have come down through the generations, as those who have borne thorns have thrust them into the hearts of others so they would join them in their pain.

What happens if a thorn is left in place and not withdrawn? The pain from it increases as infection sets in. It is the same with the thorns that have been left in place within the hearts, minds, and spirits of My precious children. Have you not seen their evidence? As a tender child is ridiculed by someone, a thorn is introduced; it is a thorn of self-doubt or, perhaps, self-hate. If there has been an assault upon the innocence of a child by way of violence or sexual perversion, a deep thorn invades this vulnerable one. There are so many ways and so many points of entry for these thorns of pain and bitterness, of dysfunction and hatred, of sadness and doubt.

Have you felt thorns in your flesh, emotions, or spirit? What action have you taken toward them? Have you shielded them? Have you denied them and their crippling effects? Have you held on to them so you would feel permission to act in kind to others? Have you been too preoccupied with the pain and with coping to even notice the sources from which they came?

What is to be done about thorns? To be in this life means you will face the hazard of thorns being directed into your being. When you have been stuck by a thorn, whether in your past or in your present, you must respond. Do not respond by grabbing a similar thorn, and then by thrusting it into the one who wounded you. Respond with a cry to be heard by My ears, a cry to My name to restore you.

Expose your woundedness to Me. Become vulnerable to My love and touch again. I shall gently extract the thorn, and I shall bring its wound to certain healing. Then, turn with forgiveness to the one who inflicted the wound upon you, and perhaps you will bring healing to the very one who caused you the pain.

There is a mystery that you must know about thorns that have been thrust upon the innocent. When the wounded one turns to Me, and asks both for forgiveness and healing for the perpetrator of the pain, an act of redemption begins. Such love and compassion bring to bear many circumstances and conditions you cannot know, but which all work toward restoration.

You have seen this before. Do you remember? It was no accident that an innocent victim was impaled with a crown of thorns. Within that crown of thorns there was the painful payment—the price for every thorn which would ever pierce My children. In the midst of that great pain came the cry of which I have spoken to you: "Forgive them." At the same time, this heart of innocence cried out, "Restore them to yourself." And it was so.

You see, the price has been paid for the thorns you bear. Give them to Me now, so I can remove them and bring you healing. Allow Me to take them, so that he who has wounded you might have a chance to be restored in your love. Will you do this thing of faith, my love, for yourself and for the others who love Me? Truly I say to you, in the New Kingdom of My love there will be no thorns, no pain, and no hazards. Until then, know that the Kingdom of God is within you; it is there for the purpose of overcoming the world's pain and ugliness. Yield to My hand. Forgive, be set free, and be restored.

REGRET

Little one, what is sad about a beautiful flower, which dies after coming to full bloom? There is no sadness or regret in such a thing. The flower did well what it was created to do. It opened itself up to the world—hiding nothing of itself. It gave up its days to declare the glory of the Creator and to give delight to My world. This is joy! This is fulfillment!

The world is filled with people whose lives show forth sadness and regret. Unlike the flowers, they have spent their days on things that have left them unfulfilled. Rather than opening themselves wide to the call given by the Creator, they have closed themselves off to My divine plan.

They have not revealed the beauty that was placed deep within them at their creation. Instead, they have refused to bloom according to their created design. They designed their own purpose and plan, which denied them the joy of fulfillment. Still in bud, their lives remained closed. Their true beauty was left unborn and unseen in the world. The days given to these unopened flowers were driven by control and self-determination. They sought to bloom for their own glory. They sported their colors to be admired and approved. They never saw the depth of glory within themselves, because they took what was never theirs, and perverted it into the ways of the world.

These who were created to be a delight in My world have become identified by their thorns rather than by their beauty of blossom, fragrance, or fruit.

Why do these, who are surrounded by sadness, believe that they live in fullness? They have not even opened themselves sufficiently to truly see the light of the "Sonshine." They have not known the loving caress of My gentle rain. They were afraid to risk exposure. Some have even surmised that if they open up themselves to My presence, they would lose their allotted days, that I would rob them. They believed that if they were to bloom they would surely wither. Staying intact meant staying in the closed-bud stage of life development.

Such a life reaches its end only to realize that the "blossom" of their days is named "regret." Things that might have been never were. Things that were presumed to be glory faded into emptiness. And what lasting impression remains behind as a witness to their lives? Bitterness, unmet dreams, and futility are their legacy. The wealth of material things has proven to be hollow and impermanent. Like eating cotton candy, it has been of no substance, disappearing quickly, tasting sweet for only a moment.

I have not created you to bring forth regret. I have created you to bring forth joyful fruit and glory for My Kingdom. I created you to open wide to the light of My love, to drink deeply of My living water.

Will these unopened buds ever realize their error and then bloom? Tragically, most do not. At their life's end, they look back to see the glory of their lives fade away. The book of their lives is filled with blank pages, and with the last stroke of the pen, they write, "REGRET." They weep and so do I.

Come, trust, yield, and open to My hand. Then, at the end of your days, we shall dance together. It will be a dance of fulfilled victory.

WEARING THE YOKE

To be in human flesh is to wear a yoke. It is only as one leaves the abode of the earth that the yoke is removed. Since this is the lot of all My children, they would do well to learn how to wear the yoke. It need not be a crushing burden, but only a reminder that My little ones still walk in the flesh.

At the beginning of creation, My children were free of any yoke. All that is in My storehouse fell freely into their possession. When the choice was made to disobey Me, however, My human creation found themselves under the yoke of consequence concerning their choice.

No longer would everything be easy. Now life on earth would consist of both work and challenge. If My child would choose to bear this yoke alone, without calling upon Me to join him or her in the pulling of the load, then the burden would indeed be heavy. However, if one would cry out and acknowledge the need for a Deliverer and a Helper in the difficult journey of life, I would be quick to respond with My help.

Some of My children are born with a more difficult yoke upon them due to the decisions and choices their parents and ancestors made. Some carry a weight forced upon them from the sinful world of the present. In either case, I am quick to lighten their load by sharing it Myself, if they would only call out to Me. Each child has the right to choose Me or not—to call out or remain silent before Me.

It is written that My yoke is easy and My burden is light. Does that mean that I carry very little of the weight? No! It means that anything that comes to Me can be carried easily upon My shoulders. As one shares My yoke, I always carry the greater weight of the burden, and I delight in doing so.

Who would choose to take the weight from My side, to make it his own? Sadly, such a choice is often made. How foolish this is, for no human creation alone can carry such a load. Too many accuse Me of piling on the weight when all along it is by their own doing that the burden comes to them.

Others have not learned how to wear the yoke. They do not wear it on the strongest place, across their shoulders. Rather, they lay it across a weak place. The neck cannot support it, no matter how stiff it is. The forehead cannot support it, no matter how strong the intellect and mind might be. The arms cannot bear it, no matter how strong the will to embrace it might be.

The yoke must be situated, placed, and positioned by Me. It must be placed upon the shoulders so that it is carried evenly on the body. In this way strength is drawn from all parts. Balance, sound footing, and even postures of rest are available to the person who bears the load in this way.

The lesson of learning how to carry the load is then followed by learning how to walk in partnership with Me. There must be no striving to beyond my pace. There must be no lagging behind either. There must be perfect agreement in our steps and in our stopping and going. When we move forward we must do so together, and when I cease moving, you must wait.

No field can ever be plowed when the oxen are not matched in their pace and movement. If the burden rests too heavily upon the weaker one, so that exhaustion occurs, the forward progress ceases. One cannot be allowed to drag the other along. If one member of the pair stops while the other advances, a stationary circle will be the result.

You were created for partnership and relationship with Me. You are to be the weaker partner who depends upon My strength and My wisdom. If you relegate to Me the secondary status, you will soon tire and fall. If you will not allow Me to be yoked with you in this life, you will advance little, and you will produce nothing eternal.

Why would you choose lonely struggle and frustrated efforts over strength and effectiveness? One reason comes rapidly forward; it is *arrogance*. Arrogance comes in the form of self-sufficiency, self-determination, and rebellion. Yes, to rebel is a statement of arrogance. In such a form of rebellion, the creature presumes to know the journey better than the Creator. Operating in this deception the created one declares that he or she needs nothing but the self and its abilities to live a meaningful life.

Put aside these things, and be yoked with Me in love. I shall be your strength. I shall make the adjustments to your load that are necessary, in accordance with the appropriate season of your life. See the fruit of being yoked with Me. As we walk together, working and carrying the load together, you shall see strength, joy in success, companionship, comfort, security, and safety arising within you.

Therefore, let go of your need to direct and control. Let go, My children, of your need to feel "all grown up" and independent. You will outgrow your need for your earthly parents, but you will never outgrow your need for Me. And I will never tire of being yoked with you in My love.

CLIMBING MOUNTAINS

So many times, little one, the day-to-day challenges of your life seem to loom in front of you like a great mountain. In the moments just prior to the ascent these questions come: Why is this so great a thing now set before me? Must I climb it? Is there an easier way to get to the road ahead?

The first step forward in any challenge is always making peace with the reality that the challenge is real, that it is truly yours, and that it is, in fact, necessary. Those who do not take this first crucial step often sit down to wait for another way to appear or for someone to come along who might carry the traveler up the mountain. In doing so, their journey stops. Soon the heat of the noonday sun will beat down on the traveler's head. His or her water supply will be depleted. The one who was called to embark on the journey soon dries up and withers away.

However, if the first steps up the mountain are accepted and chosen, progress will soon be made. Along the way of the climb, many choices will appear. Is it easier to climb by way of the carved stone steps—the path built by great efforts of those who have passed this way before? Or should the narrow, direct path be the way? Only a few others have walked upon this trail. It is obviously more narrow and uncertain. Is there a shortcut that can be made through the virgin forest and underbrush? No one, it appears, has ever chosen this way. The dangers involved with this choice seem greater, but then, perhaps the climb would be significantly shorter this way.

Sometimes it is best to tackle a great task through methods that have been used by others who have faced similar situations. The safety of proven strategies is far greater and the comfort they provide is surer. The already-tested way has many resting places, allowing the climb to be more comfortable and less tiresome, even though it may actually be longer.

The less-clear path may be the best learning experience, however. The traveler who journeys along this way will have to discover where it may be safe to walk and where the hazards are. The footing may be less sure, so that the stress of the climb may prove to be greater. And yet, this may be of greater overall benefit to the climber with regard to other journeys that may still lie ahead.

The greatest uncertainty lies in the climb where no others have ventured before. For such routes there are no human maps and no road signs to follow. In the dense forest there is less light and greater, unseen dangers. Along this climb, the compass, the rope, and the knife are vital tools for the climber. The compass ensures that he or she will be able to travel in the right direction. The rope makes it possible to cross over chasms that may appear. The knife defends against poisonous serpents and may be used to help provide food during the arduous journey.

On this route, the climber has the singular opportunity to experience the blessings of overcoming in the face of great odds. Similarly, in the journey of faith you will need to meet a variety of challenges, according to My recommendations. Always remember that I know what course to take. I always know what is needful for you.

Though it takes greater strength and skill to forge a path, others will benefit from your efforts. Sometimes you will need many tools and weapons to conquer the mountain. At other times you will need only strength and persistence.

Ask Me to show you how to climb the mountain. I will direct and equip you. Always remember to keep climbing. You were designed to be an overcomer in Me. If you choose to stay at the foot of the mountain, then the mountain will defeat you. It may even destroy your journey.

Your surrender to defeat ensures your failure and your loss. Do not be overconfident in your own strength and in your own ability. Listen to My way, and follow Me in obedience. When I call for you to rest, simply stop and rest. I will never set before you too great a task for you to accomplish. I will never allow so great an obstacle to come before you that you will not be able to surmount it. Trust Me. Do not trust your eyes. Trust and climb. Do not trust your reason or understanding.

When you have defeated the mountain, you will have acquired new learning and strength. Those things will become a part of you and will remain with you. They will serve you greatly when the next mountain appears before you.

You were created to achieve victory in Me. You were made to be a dweller on the high ground. Truly, from the heights many new and otherwise unseen things can be viewed and understood.

Come! Do not be afraid of the mountain. I could remove it easily if it were My will to do so. Trust My hand and My purpose with regard to the mountain you face. As it remains before you, I shall transform it into a gift. In the process, I will transform you into the gifted.

THUNDER AND STORM

Little one, what does the sound of thunder indicate? It signals the onset of a disturbance. It signals an environmental conflict producing an oncoming storm. A storm is caused when an atmosphere of high temperature conflicts with a mass of cooler air. These two systems battle with each other in their attempt to determine the prevailing weather condition.

Hot air is lighter than the cold air, so the hot air has the superior position. As the two temperature systems meet in the battle of a storm, the system that survives the encounter declares that a change has occurred. The hotter temperature has cooled down, and the cooler temperature has become warmer. Both air masses have been affected and modified by the encounter.

Whenever those who are "hot" in My Spirit meet with believers who are "cool" or "cold," there will be a disturbance. There will be clashing, noise, and a storm will result. Each will seek to hold the predominant position. Those who are on higher ground will have the advantage.

The presence of My Word and the presence of active, unconditional love put one upon higher ground. However, even he who stands upon the higher ground will never be able to overcome the coolness of the other by means of force. He or she must mingle the fire of My Spirit with the heat of love in order to modify the cool fear of the other person. The one containing a greater warmth must present a climate of submission to My will and way instead of yielding to the demand for control within the other. After the encounter, there will be a modification in the lives of both individuals. The "cold" ones will have become somewhat warmer by the contact, and the "burning hot" one will have offered up some of his or her heat to warm the other.

The sound of thunder is frightening to many, especially to small children. Similarly, the sound of conflict within My Body that occurs when the two varying temperatures collide is the instigator of fear in My people. I do not see it as the major threat they perceive, however. I see it as the herald of change. If the two never were to meet, there would be no storm. There would be only a quiet and dangerous separation. I need these two extremes to meet each other. Indeed, I call for it to happen.

Do not hear the oncoming thunder and then say, "This is a bad thing that is coming." Say only, "There is change in the air. A new climate of understanding is coming." True, flesh can maneuver My Spirit to a limited degree. But it can never eliminate My power to bring change. Can a person hold back the thunder? Does its sound cease to be by covering one's ears? No! It will come, and My direction will be in it and over it.

After the cooling of the storm, the temperatures will again rise. However, this time, it will be the two, mingling temperatures that will rise together.

Allow Me to direct the mix and the timing. It shall be done well. Fear not! Do not try to control the prevailing climate of My Spirit: Give Me the conditions of the meeting and all those who are involved. I shall swirl them together at just the right moment and make something new and fresh from the confrontation. There shall be a flash of great power and light. There shall be the great roar of new creation. There shall be the sweet fragrance of unity. Then the rain will come.

OSTRICHES

Consider My creation of the ostrich, little one. The ostrich is magnificent in My eyes. Human eyes, on the other hand, may see the ostrich as being ridiculous. Nonetheless, these birds are filled with lessons for those who are open to them and seek them.

Everything I create brings a teaching—a revelation of deeper truths and realities. Is it surprising to find that which the world sees as foolish is, in fact, a rich, spiritual treasure? I choose that which appears to be foolish in order to confound the wise and the arrogant.

Why would I create a bird that is so large and seemingly so disproportionate? Why would I create such a big body with tiny wings? Why would I give a bird a hissing and a squawking voice instead of a song? Surely a human engineer would have been wiser and done better, some may reason. What was I thinking when I created the ostrich with these features? Did I leave the task to a committee of angels?

Consider the lessons to be learned from the ostrich. A bird without flight would seem helpless. Yet, this is not the case with the ostrich. Its long legs and its long neck lift its eyes above many things. Such a vantage point is useful when it comes to seeing danger at a distance. Once seen, the threat may be greeted in two ways. The bird can run on the powerful legs I have provided for it. No bird is able to run away faster. The second option is to attack the danger by using those same capable legs. If the foe does not run off, it can be met effectively in combat by way of the ostrich's mighty kicks.

While the ostrich's wings cannot lift it high above the threat, they do provide balance, enabling easy maneuverability while attacking and defending. As the feet advance, the beak is always ready to bite. The voice both sends forth an alarm to the others and at the same time evokes fear into the attacker's heart.

Now, was I not wise in the way I designed the ostrich? Even the weakness of the ostrich is a valuable object lesson. Have you perceived it? Such a powerful and great creature would be fearless of small things, would it not? And yet, the ostrich is easily surprised and startled into terror by the smallest unexpected or unknown sound or presence.

It is quick to seek a hiding place, as its heart pounds in panic. In the soft folds of the sand, the startled ostrich buries its head. That which startled it is now unseen and unheard. In the understanding of the ostrich, it is gone, and it is no longer a threat.

In many ways, My human creation resembles the ostrich. I have made My children both powerful and capable. By My gifting, they can defend against the enemy. They can see the advancing foe by way of the high vision I've provided by my Spirit. They can move quickly to safety or move against the enemy, causing him to flee. In battle, they are well equipped with the weapons of My Spirit, if they would only pick them up and use them. Using the wings of My Spirit, they can balance and maneuver well in every fray. Each one has a voice to shout the alarm to others, and each one has a cry with which to confuse and frighten that which would attempt to subdue them.

With such equipping, why would any of My children fear? And yet, fear continually immobilizes so many of My children. Walking in preoccupation, or in self-occupation, they can be surprised and startled by the slightest rustling about them. Forgetting their available resources and gifting, they scurry to find safety. They run to places where there is no safety, thinking that this will give them security. Some "bury their heads" in the sands of the past. Others "bury their heads" in institutions or in traditions. Many retreat to their own understanding or to the understandings of other people. There is no safety in these things. Human understanding is far too inadequate, as are all other human resources. Has the threat gone away as a result of hiding? No!

And what about the threat? What is the true nature of the perceived threat? What if the stirring—the rustle—the sound in your ear is Me? What if I have drawn closer to you in order to seek you and to touch you in love? Would I be a threat? Sadly, for some I am a threat, particularly if I move too close to them. My drawing close to them threatens their world and their understanding of who I am and what I am expected to do. It threatens their very spiritual understandings and the false premises they cling to. Why? If I would love beyond all others, would I not also long to be closer than all others?

So, now would you have Me touch you? Would it be in an awesome grandeur that is worthy of My status, or would it be in a simple, unpredictable style of yours? I make Myself known, and I touch people in the ways I choose, not in the ways of human convention.

Does this offend you? Does it threaten your need for distance and control? In these things, make note of the arrogance of your heart. How would you demand your God to appear and touch you? Be careful, little one. Throughout the generations, I have come near to My children, but only to the humble of heart who were willing to receive Me in the form I chose to reveal to them. Those who were willing to receive Me were enabled to embrace me. What if Moses had said, "I shall not speak to a bush, for surely a great God would only speak out of the fire of a mountain?" The bush was one choice I made to reveal Myself—the mountain was another face of revelation yet to come.

I can *choose* to present Myself in great glory or in quiet simplicity. I can choose to touch one's mind in gentle revelation or touch one's body in humbling, vibrating convulsions.

Ask Me to come and touch you, and I will. Dictate how I *must* appear or legislate when I should move upon you, and you will be distanced from Me. The distance will be of your choosing, not Mine. Consider these things carefully, My child. If you fear *deception,* be an open seeker of *My truth.* Your own preconceptions leave you vulnerable to deception. Listen for My voice and watch for My presence. If your fear causes you to hide in the sands of human things or in the precepts of this world's understandings, surely, as I walk by, you will miss My touch.

SHEARING

The heat has come, and the cold of winter has passed. What was necessary covering for the body during the chill can now be put aside. There is no need for a coat or a hat now. They can be easily removed and stored away. But what about those things which are a part of you, those things that are attached to you? Can the sheep remove his winter garment? When too long or too thick, can the hair growing from your scalp be removed like a hat? No! So, how does one remove that which is grown like fleece into garments? It is necessary to call in another person who has the proper tools to remove them.

The sheep needs the shepherd with shears to carefully cut away its heavy coat. Shearing must be done with great skill to avoid injury to the sheep. But what about a man or a woman? Can a person cut his own hair without a mirror? It is far easier, and done more effectively, when a barber is given the work. He who has the tools and the skills can do the work quickly, without injury to the one being trimmed.

Consider now those things in a person's history, attitudes, understanding, or behaviors which have become unnecessary, stifling garments. These things no longer bring comfort to the individual. They now can bring suffocation and even a loss of consciousness due to heat prostration.

How few of My children are willing to come to Me for the shearing they so desperately need. Without a mirror and with blade in hand, they begin to chop and to cut. They do not have the necessary vision or tools to do this work. They have no training and skill. Once they are aware that the garment clinging to them is too great a weight upon them, they often seek to remove it immediately. Foolishly, they often seek to remove that which has grown to be a part of them, as if it were only a sweater.

If only they would seek Me rather than attempting to use their own methods and understandings. I am the Master Shearer. I know exactly how to cut away, what to cut away, and what to retain. I know what skills are needed to keep My sheep from injury. Let Me wield the shears. Do not allow another person to do this job, unless I am guiding the hand of that person. Seek My wisdom before entrusting your shearing to another.

Why does the shearing need to be done? It is for health of the sheep and for its comfort, so that fresh air and light can reach the body of the sheep and the load upon its back and feet might be made much lighter. These are some of the reasons, but yet, there is a more important reason. That which has become the "garment" of one's life experience and is no longer necessary or helpful, may need to come off to assist another person. Again, the pain of one's life, once removed and washed, can become hope and warmth for another little one who may now be shivering in the dark and cold in hopelessness or shame.

You see, the stories of My healed and freed ones can comfort others who suffer. A naked, shamed lamb can be covered in the blanket of your victory over similar nakedness. The pain, sheared away and woven into victory, can serve as support and direction for others who are overburdened, for those who have lost sight of the Shepherd and for those who have hidden from Him. Your story of love and victory brings forth in these others the trust that is needed to return them to the Shepherd's care.

The woolly coat of the sheep in the springtime needs to come off both for his comfort and for the use of another. That which has become an encumbrance to one can be taken apart, washed, and knitted into something new—something of great beauty. The new blanket or sweater is, indeed, made of the same material. It still is wool. But now it is in a different and more useful form for the present season. That which was uncomfortable in the heat of springtime can become warmth for those who will shiver when the cold comes again. First, the heavy, wool fleece must be transformed so that it can be used in the winter.

Do not try to cut away your own garments of burden and history, little one. Do not despise nor discard the matted clumps they form. Let Me carefully remove them, cleanse them, and remake them upon My loom, so that the relief of one can become a blessing to many.

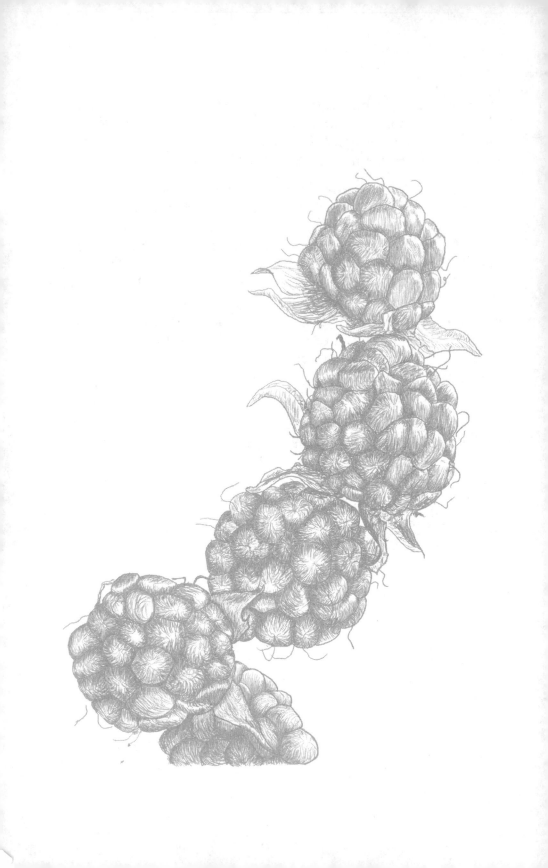

HARVESTING RASPBERRIES

How lovely are the bushes decked out in the beautiful red of the raspberries. In the morning sun, they summon the appetites of the birds circling above them. But these delicious treasures are for the delight of My human children this morning. Who will venture out early to gather them while they still remain on the bushes? It must be one who will be unafraid of thorns and mosquitoes—one who will put aside the leisure of the morning in order to labor for the harvest.

Do you see how the unripe berries cling to their attachment, little one? Their harvest is based upon timing. If they are plucked too soon, they will lack the juice and sweetness that come from being ripe in My timing. To pick them prematurely is both a struggle and a disappointment. It is a struggle to detach them without injury and that would seem to be frustration enough, but then to have them in hand and to find out that they lack full flavor and quality would be an even greater disappointment.

It is the same with the harvesting of My human "fruit." When well-intentioned harvesters move too quickly upon one who is not yet ripe and full in My timing, those who would gather are left frustrated and disappointed with the fruit. Forced to be claimed too soon, the one being harvested can actually be damaged and be denied the full sweetness of his season. I will always instruct those who will listen about the ways of the harvest. He who planted the seeds, the One who knows both the vines and the seasons, must be the One who will declare the time of harvest. Listen for My directions as you patiently watch for the sign of ripeness.

Harvest of the berries, when ripe, must occur swiftly to avoid being lost to the circling birds who would prey upon them. So, too, it is with the gathering of My children in the harvest of their souls. The enemy of the Gardener comes and waits for the moment of choice ripeness, which is his opportunity to prey upon them. See how the birds neglect the unripe berries? Only those berries that are ready and ripe for harvest are targeted by them.

In the same way, watch when you see My enemy circling above, for it is then that he is ready to dive upon My ripening children. Move quickly to snatch them up into My hands, as I call to you. When the enemy appears boldly, prepare to move boldly to save them.

Look carefully underneath the leaves in order to harvest the fruit. Don't look only on the surface, where you can easily see the plump, ripe berries. There you will find many who have been neglected and now wait, overfull with juice and splendor. Many will ripen here, too far from notice, and they will fall to the ground to rot or to be devoured by the slugs. They would have achieved ripeness and harvest potential while remaining unseen and unnoticed. They would be excluded from the harvest because of the lack of attentive harvesters.

Look for My hidden children, little one. Look for those who wait in private silence, on the very edge of life itself. Stoop and look for them lovingly. These have ripened by My grace, even without the benefit of the present "Sonshine." These, too, are sweet and pleasing to Me. So, hunt carefully. Be ever watchful for these. Some have come to a place of ripeness without the benefit of exposure to the things of My Kingdom and without the truths of My Kingdom. My Spirit has far-reaching influence. Do not discount what I can do to prepare My own, even when they are unseen by you.

What about the thorns? Those who would gather ripe berries for the table need to be aware of the thorns and they need to be unafraid of them. A timid harvester who is bent upon comfort and ease would gather little. To reach in among the thorns, to capture the precious treasures that are clinging to the branches—the fruit awaiting touch—requires courage and self-surrender. The goal of the harvest overshadows the threat of pain.

When gathering My children to Me, harvester, you must be surrendered to both the labor and to the personal cost of the labor. Woundedness frequently occurs when one gathers both ripe berries and My human treasure, as well. Reach out! Surrender yourself to the harvest, and do not pull back from the tearing of the thorns. Do not retreat from the harvest in order to avoid its pain. Stretch out into the threat, guided by My hand and by My Word. I shall be the Healer of your wounds, and I shall be the Restorer of the torn places. I carefully pull out the thorns that get embedded in the flesh. Trust Me! The pain shall never overshadow the joy you will receive from the gathering of My little ones. I promise!

Do the mosquitoes within the berry patch annoy you? They come to hover where there is moisture. The water in the soil feeds My ripening berries, and it also draws the attention of the mosquitoes. They are merely an annoyance, though, not a hazard. Cover yourself with mosquito repellent before you go forth into the berry patch.

Likewise, when you are about to harvest My human fruit for the glory of My Kingdom, be careful to cover yourself. Cover yourself with My Word, with prayer, with fasting, and with praise. These things will drive away the annoyances. In fact, the hovering swarms will not even be noticed as you take part in the joy of harvesting.

A gatherer of raspberries may be thwarted in the plucking by the mere sight of the swarm. Do not look at or consider the size of the swarm. Do not be forestalled by its appearance. Cover yourself and then look only upon the awaiting fruit. Never focus upon the mosquitoes. Do not give heed to their deafening and threatening buzz.

Upon occasion, I will call specially chosen harvesters to go out into the deep woods, to gather from the wild bushes. These will encounter the bear and the snake who freely inhabit these areas. These predators of the wild berries claim their right to feed upon them in their territory. Do not venture out into the deep woods, however, believing yourself properly equipped for this harvest. Only those who have been taught the way of the bear and the snake, those who listen with the greatest attentiveness to My voice are selected to claim the wild ones. Only those who have been taught the hidden path and the dark secrets of the forest may venture here. Stand ready to receive this precious harvest, as it is lovingly carried from the darkened woods. Stand ready to bind up the wounds of the harvesters, for these may suffer much for the sake of this harvest. Stand ready to celebrate the victory of this claimed treasure.

When the harvest of berries is complete, when the table is set, displaying the fruit, and when the season of harvest is over, there is always great rejoicing. Likewise, when My human harvest is complete and when My table is set, displaying the bounty, when the season of harvest has ended, all of heaven shall rejoice. The wounds, the thorns, the slugs, and the mosquitoes of this life shall then be forgotten. Together we shall rejoice and delight in the bounty. Together we shall rejoice *forever*!

SONGBIRDS

There are many species of songbirds, little one. Some are joyously bright with color, while others are nearly unnoticed in their humble garb. Did I make the bright ones with more love? Did I create the dull in appearance with less favor? No! I create according to My purpose.

Some are needed to bring joy and celebration. Others are needed to join My children in their pain, bringing simple comfort in companionship. When one is downcast and suffering, a bright bird is too sharp a contrast, and this only intensifies the pain. One of simpler color can be embraced and received. Rejection is more intense in the presence of the flamboyant. Comfort and acceptance are absorbed more effectively in the presence of the humble.

When you find one of My children in a time of celebration, adorn the full spectrum of color into your soul. Wear it openly. When you find a brother or sister in deep pain, subdue your flamboyance. Put on a garment which is lacking in soulish, demonstrative color. As a servant, put aside your need to be noticed and unrestrained. Step down into a humble holding of the other. Wrap your wings of peace around the suffering one. Be his or her strength and shelter, rather than a celebration or a dance. Gently pull out the thorn. Bring healing oil and nurse the one back to his or her own strength and joy in Me. Then celebrate the restoration. First, put upon him or her the garments of praise, then adorn yourself with them. Enter into another's pain, not to injure your-self or to yield up your deep joy, only to place your joy in the quietness of your inner being where it can move in power through your quietness in Me.

Notice the songs of My birds. Do all birds make music? No. Some who are flamboyant in color, can only squawk. Yet, the most humbly adorned often have the sweetest song. Why would I do such a thing? Sometimes a bright appearance would overshadow a song's message. The eyes are too easily overwhelmed and are too tightly focused upon that which is brightest. The song would be lost to the ears due to the obsession of the eyes. How best do you hear that which you would stretch to hear? You close your eyes, so that your focus is solely upon hearing.

Do not be overwhelmed or distracted by what you see in My children. Do not be seduced into believing that greater favor goes to the beautiful and richly adorned. Some of My most valuable songs come from the lips of My poor and simple children, those who draw no attention to the eye, except, perhaps, to pity. Listen to the words of these precious ones. Listen to the songs I have placed within their hearts and lips. My world needs to hear their music. Let it be heard first in your ears of both flesh and spirit. Close tightly your eyes of flesh, and listen to the song that arises in these precious children by My Spirit.

WITHIN THE FOLD

Little one, satan seeks to sift each of My children as wheat. He seeks to create doubt, division, blindness, and a spirit of redress. Every dark and evil thing comes from him, and each is designed to inflict My children.

I am the Shepherd. I call My sheep. They follow My voice, and they dwell in safety. But the false voice comes and it often mimics My own voice. If My children follow that voice, they are led astray.

In My sheepfold there is protection for My sheep. When the sheep hear My voice, they will move together, as they confirm that the voice is Mine. However, if there is a sheep that is standing apart from the fold, away from Me, and he or she also hears a voice, the sheep has no one to either confirm or deny its source. Lone sheep are prone to guessing, and guessing can be deadly, indeed.

On cold nights the sheep in the fold may huddle together, sharing their inner warmth as protection against the harsh chill.

Each one adds to the total warmth, creating a great, comfortable heat. Alone, however, a solitary sheep can freeze.

Alone, a sheep can easily wander away from safety, because he or she is occupied and distracted by grazing. In wandering, he or she may fall into a crevice. In such a case, he who hears or sees the predicament to sound an alarm with a chorus of bleating? Much pain occurs in the lonely, injured, fright-filled sheep who is waiting for help.

I have created the sheepfold for My sheep to provide them with safety, comfort, and fellowship with Me and with the rest of the flock. Yet, how many sheep would choose to remain outside the fold, feeling it to be too restrictive and too confining? Oh, what benefits they deny themselves. Within the fold there always is an abundance of love, warmth, and protection.

Think upon the expressions of this love. In a time of sorrow, one who loves may cry your tears with you, even to the point of tasting the salt within them. In this way, strength is added to your weakness, as the pain is divided and borne by more than one. The strength of another is added to your own. Only love can dilute, diminish, or delete pain. When there is no strength in one member, the strength of another coming alongside enables the journey to continue.

In a time of confusion, one within the flock can, in love, offer up clarity and wisdom that has been given by Me. When the fires of anger rage, words of compassion and love can diminish their potential to burn. Open wounds can be cleansed and irrigated for healing by the generous flow of tears from others who love.

I did not create My children for solitude. I create eternal ties. Have you not felt the cords that bind hearts together, adding strength, even when time and space bring physical distance? Have you not felt your balance being maintained even in a state of dizziness, as two of sound footing stood by, holding you on each side?

Are not lessons more easily and joyfully learned in the company of those who love? Lessons learned in isolation have a singular sting.

To each of My children I give gifts. Each is complementary to others. To make a cake requires many ingredients. If you lack any of the ingredients, you must obtain them from another. Together you will complete the task, and together you will enjoy the taste of the completed work. However, if you would seek to complete the recipe with some elements missing, the outcome would be incomplete at best, and disastrously inedible at worst.

Each person in My flock brings a part of the blessing to the whole creation. Unity, sharing, and embracing are important parts of My way. As I fellowship with My Father and the Spirit, so you, too, have been created for fellowship—first with Us, and then with others.

WHEAT AND TARES

Truly, the harvest time is drawing near, little one. Even now the wheat and the tares are growing together toward maturity. While the enemy has previously planted the tares to choke out all the wheat, it shall not be so. I allow this deception to continue. I allow the false doctrine and the false prophesy to be uttered.

They shall come forth, side by side, both true and false, so that those who choose to discern will do so and those who choose to use their own reason and intellect to understand will stumble. Those who are deceived must learn to yield up their need to be fascinated and dazzled by the world's way. Those who see only weeds, when there is also wheat standing with them, must also learn to discern. These, too, are greatly deceived.

Which is the greater sin, to say that those who are ungodly are godly, or to say that the godly are ungodly? Both have a high cost, but the latter has the greater cost. Those who would pull up the weeds, careless of the wheat, will greatly lessen the harvest. It is

My wisdom to allow the two to grow side by side, together, until the time of harvest.

Those who discern My Spirit will clearly see both the wheat and the tares. They will tend the wheat, being careful not to disturb the roots. Wait for the harvest! Do not pull at the weeds prematurely, for if you do so, the wheat will die by being uprooted. Truly, I say the tares will be sorted out first at the harvest, so that the wheat can be gathered and celebrated.

Harvesters and watchers of the field do not focus upon the size and density of the tares! Continue to plant good seed. Continue to tend it with prayer and nurturing. You are to be planters, not pullers, in these days. In due time, I will commission the pulling, but I alone must commission it. I do not need field workers and watchers to do My job. In their zeal to help Me, they lack wisdom and knowledge of My timing.

The planter of the tares would love to coax you into a fiery zeal of pulling. This would serve his purpose of uprooting and destroying the good seed that is now growing. It would cause the destruction of the harvest's bounty.

So, stay to your tasks, and do not expand your role beyond My commissioning. I am the owner of the field. You are not. The barns are mine, not yours. I do not need your unwise ambition. I need your watchful discernment and your obedience.

Behold, the wheat continues to mature quickly in these days. The harvest will soon be at hand. Watch. Plant. Moisten with living water. And wait upon My call to signal harvest. I will order My workers to gather the tares into bundles. Soon it will come. Meanwhile, do not defend the wheat in one field by uprooting the wheat with the tares in another field in an attempt to keep the tares from spreading. Instead, defend the wheat with prayer. Prayer is like poison to the tares. In its presence, the tares wither and the wheat thrives.

Liberally cover the ripening fields with prayer while you continue to plant good seed. My eyes are upon these things—*all* these things. Trust Me and obey. You, who are the substance of the wheat, as well as the tender of the wheat, obey My call. In the final accounting, it shall please Me to share the bounty of the harvest with you, in the eternity of My Kingdom.

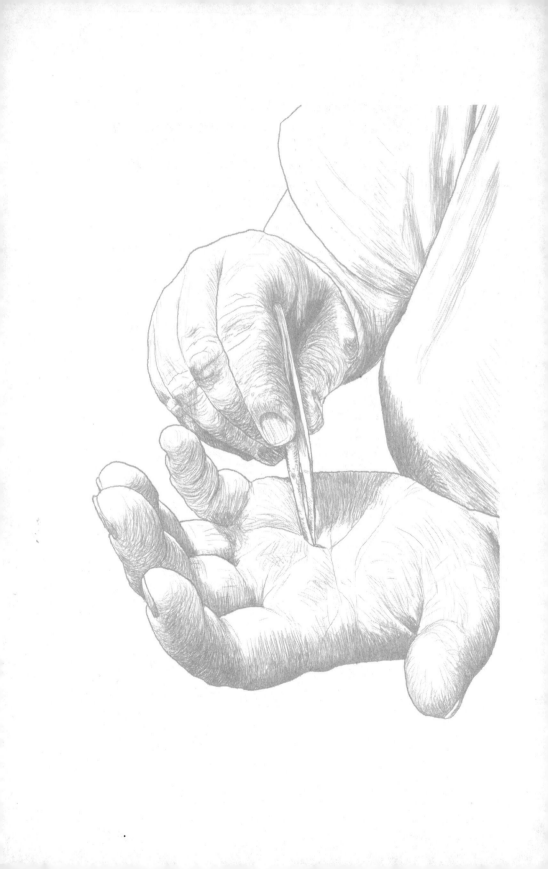

REMOVING SPLINTERS

Little one, so many of My children are inflicted with embedded splinters in their flesh, soul, or spirit. They pull against them, they strive to hide them, or they struggle to ignore them and the pain they cause. The substance of these splinters is much like wood; it is both soft and sharp. To grab the edge of the splinter will free only a fragment of it. Splintering often occurs in the piece itself. The larger part remains far beneath the surface. Removing a fragment brings little relief, and it often intensifies one's frustration and helplessness. The pain will increase with time, as infection sets in. Anger and impatience are likely to fester along with the infection.

How do you remove a fragmenting, embedded splinter from a finger? Is it accomplished in the same way one would be removed from a heart? Careful, surgical probing and digging by one who possesses gentleness, vision, and skill is needed. While not being insensitive to the cries of pain, the one lending the aid must not be overwhelmed by it nor withdraw from the work because of it. Even the cries of "STOP!" must not be heeded. For to stop would mean to give the wound over to more serious infection. Hold and tend the emotions overflowing from the one in pain, but do not change course. Go after the "heart" of the splinter. Remove pieces blocking the way, as you go after the main piece. Do this carefully until you have fully grasped and withdrawn it. To stop short of full removal of every piece is to leave a hazard in place.

How much more serious is a splinter of the heart—a wound in the emotions made by embedded cruelty. A formidable splinter within the heart often consists of an accumulation of words, actions, assumptions, judgments, lies, and anger. If the offending fragments are at a surface level, it is far easier to remove them and to medicate the wound for healing. If the impaled flesh has been so deeply assaulted that the edge of the splinter is barely visible, however, a great work must take place. The surrounding flesh must be disrupted and cut away, so that the grasping tool may have a clear path to do its work or removal. In the cutting away, there may be bleeding and fear mingled with the pain.

In such a case, the mind may be quick to say, "The pain of removal is too great. I can live with the injury! Don't touch the area, for the splinter may be impacted by the touch, causing it to go yet deeper. Leave it alone!"

All of these impulses speak of retreat in fear and in frustration. They speak of despair and of deep sadness. Only one Physician can direct this procedure. Even as a healer in training sits and operates under the careful direction and supervision of an experienced teacher, so do I have My own, who operate by My guidance. Not a move can be made on assumption or by observation alone. These servants must follow precise instructions and be obedient to My every command. These procedures can be successfully done; they *must* be carried out.

Seek Me first! I will choose the hands of healing to hold your wound, to cut carefully, to remove the splinter, and to pour in the healing oil once the extraction is complete.

Trust Me! Trust the ones I train and send to you. Accept no counterfeits! Much is at stake. Much is to be risked and gained. Remember, in Me there is always gain. *Come!* Bring your wounds and your embedded splinters of pain for Me to see. Do not hide them away in terror of the procedure. I shall not belittle your pain. I shall never be careless or rough. Nor shall I ever inflict unnecessary suffering, or condemn your fear. Ask for the gift of trust. Come, raise up your hands in supplication and your heart in trust. I shall bring forth both healing and comfort. Come!

DRUMBEATS

The galley ships of old moved across the face of the water by the power of many oars. But what is the use of 100 oars that do not row in unity? If each oarsman was to pull and lift according to his own desire, little movement would be accomplished. It would matter very little if those who would row were well-equipped with matching oars and with strong muscles. Unity would be the key. Even if one oarsman were mighty in physical strength and the others were unable to match his strength, the ship would still move forward if true unity were empowering it.

To ensure the power of unity and to maximize the effectiveness of their efforts, it was necessary to have a drummer on board. This man would evenly and relentlessly pound out a steady beat to which rhythm the oarsmen would pull. Each thrust of the oars made in this unity would propel the ship forward. There was no question as to when to pull, lift, or rest. The beats of the drum would call out the proper action, leading to a steady flow of unity.

There is great strength in unity, little one. Whether it is unity that is based in good or in evil, there is always more strength in efforts that are united. Those whom I have called together to do My work have been called to unity. Why, then, does their "ship of faith" or their ministry flounder in the water? They have a drumbeat to follow. Both My Spirit and My Word call out the beat. Can they not hear it? What other sounds fill their ears? Are their hearts unsubmitted to My authority? It is so, for each one is so steadfastly independent that none will obey the drumbeat.

Those who were meant to row often rise out of their seats to seize the mallets and to release the oars. Who, then, will row? Some rise from their position to peer out the windows of the galley in order to see where the ship is taking them. Rather than trusting the Captain, they want to be sure of the direction for themselves. Perhaps they want to influence it by protesting the course to the Captain.

Some ignore the drummer, as they look out the window in their musings, enjoying the feeling of leisure in this position. Those who remain at the oars struggle to move the ship. They were never meant to do this task alone. However, in the desire to make up for those who have abandoned their task, these faithful ones try to move the ship alone. In their efforts, they succumb to exhaustion and defeat.

I am the Captain of this ship that is known as "the Body of Messiah." I use the drum to pound out the necessary beat. I call out the command to rest, to row, or to feed. Truly, I say to you, a battle lies ahead. If you will not heed the gentle drumbeat of the quiet waters, how will you ever move together in greater unity and at a quickened beat when the battle begins? Where will your victory be then?

Practice heeding the drumbeat now. Grow to love its sounds. Follow it with exact precision. Do not look to those around you to direct your actions. Listen only to the beat of the drum. Do not look around to see who is pulling his weight, and who is leaning upon the oars. This is the work of the Captain. Your obedience, your focus is to be upon the Captain's call, as it is transmitted through the drumbeats. Do not leave your post to see where I am directing you. Only row ahead. Do not attempt to seize the mallets, to initiate your own rhythm for the ship to follow. Only listen and be obedient.

Learn this now, for the time of battle approaches. Much is at stake in the looming conflict. Dig your oars deeply into the water and pull at My command. Then, when the enemy comes, you will be well-disciplined and strong. Listen to My drumbeats now and *obey*.

PERFECT LOVE

Be perfect, as your Father in heaven is perfect. Is this too big an imperative, little one? What does it mean to be perfect in this way? Does it mean that you are to be like the Most High God, absolutely without error in any form? No, for that would be impossible for you.

To be in human flesh upon a fallen world means that you will occasionally walk in error. The perfection of which I am speaking *is* attainable for you. To "be perfect," is to be set apart, to be separate, to be unlike the world in the way in which you love.

Absolute holiness in all things is reserved only for deity. Even Job, in his outstanding list of accomplishments, fell short, in so far as he was unable to see his own subtle arrogance. No one is like Adonai. And yet, by the indwelling presence of the Spirit of Adonai, a form of perfection—true holiness—is possible for you.

What is the chief characteristic of Adonai? *Love.* As the Spirit lays hold of My possession in you—your heart—you can be changed to love in My holy way. The empowerment to do so comes from Me. I will enable you to make correct choices and to practice loving as I love. Even as My love is unconditional, it is holy in nature. As your love becomes unconditional, it will take upon itself My quality of love and conform to My character.

Do I choose to love or is it My nature? You cannot fully embrace such a mystery. Suffice it to say that I made love My all-encompassing reality. Those who truly embrace Me, embrace My love. Those who truly embrace My love are transformed by it, into My very nature and My practice of loving. Does that speak clarity to your understanding, or is it too great a concept for you to grasp?

The very thing that gives My true children their greatest distinction is not just that they know and declare who I Am. It is the nature of My being living in and through them. It is their ability to love unconditionally. These do not love to be loved in return. They do not seek any gain from loving, only the joy of giving away who they are in Me. In doing so, they give away portions of Me to others, so that those portions may grow within another.

Do you now see how the process works? To love those who love you is a comfortable thing. It is easily given to carnal man to do this. This is so, because I created My human children at the very beginning to be lovers. They were designed to speak of Me within them. However, when the holiness of the human creation was tainted by sin, so also did the love I imparted to them become tainted. It could no longer flow freely. It could be withheld and manipulated. Designed to be eternally warm with the heat of My love beneath it, human love soon turned cold, due to the priority that was given to sin.

Ah, but here is the turning point for My own true children. Those who have chosen Me have made Me their priority instead of sin. Here is their victory, as well. For against such loving, there is no effective weapon. Every accusation raised up against it will be false, even if, at the time, it is not proven so.

Who can stand against such perfect love being raised up from My imperfect children? As this loving without condition, regardless of cost, is born in My reborn children, they know My perfection in their lives. They walk not only in My image, but also in My heart.

Even as the world cannot understand My love, so also it cannot be anything but confounded by this perfection in My children. Nevertheless, even misunderstood and often rejected, this love of My perfection issues forth, declaring My glory, bringing down strongholds, and adding to My Kingdom.

Therefore, be *perfect*, as your Father in heaven is perfect. Together we shall celebrate this perfection, and we shall add to it a great abundance to fill up all of eternity.

BLEMISHES

How much imperfection do you tolerate, little one? How much do you tolerate in yourself, in others, in outcomes? Does this differ according to the specific people involved? Does it vary according to the circumstances? Consider these questions seriously. In their answers you will discover such things as arrogance, compromise, and grace.

I intend for My children to have no tolerance of evil. Is all imperfection to be considered evil—something to be eliminated—something to war against?

How blessed you are that I am just, that I do not tolerate evil in any form. And yet, how blessed are you, as well, that I have compassion for imperfection, for all My human creation is a reality of functioning imperfection. Only One clothed in human flesh has been perfect always and in every way. There have never been and there will never be any others who are completely perfect while this world remains.

Who is to judge imperfection? By what measure is it determined? I once had two perfect children. They had no flaws and no blemishes in body, mind, or spirit. War was declared against their holy, perfect creation by My enemy. After he was able to spoil that perfection in My children, he began insisting that without it they would *always* be unworthy. His efforts try to bring destruction to My children at every moment. How interesting that he rails against My perfection, and yet he accuses My children for their lack of perfection. You see, he cannot tolerate My grace. That I would love those who decline My love goads him. That I would reestablish a perfect human and a spotless sacrifice through the Messiah enrages him.

It does so, because these truths neutralize his false claim that reclamation is not possible. This enemy feeds upon brokenness, and he dines upon condemnation. Where My children are blemished in body, mind, or spirit, he raises up a tirade of attack in order to intensify their pain, weakness, and sense of helplessness. He is the opposite of the Restorer. He is the one who defaces and desecrates, and he delights in doing so.

Where does this leave My little ones? It leaves them in fear of their imperfections. Some even go into hiding in order to cover up their nakedness. Still others take up the role of becoming an ally to the accuser. They hasten to point out the imperfections in others in order to avoid their own inspection. How sad that they would live and believe in such defeat. How tragic that they would propagate it in others, as well.

Through My eyes blemishes and imperfections are seen as opportunities. For where there is imperfection, My perfection can intervene and reclaim. Where there are blemishes caused by unlearned things, I can teach. Where there has been bruising and scarring, I can do the work of healing and recreating.

You see, My way is always in the direction of increase of all that is holy. My way is to increase shalom which is true wholeness. I am always the antidote to My enemy's poisons. When My enemy takes away, I move to give back. Where My adversary brings ugliness, I seek to bring forth beauty.

Have you not seen those of My children who are hideous in body? Those who are willing to receive My love, have birthed great beauty in spirit that overshadows any and all ugliness. Those who function amidst brokenness, with Me as their Source can evidence My wholeness within them. The ways of My Kingdom will always be the opposite of satan's kingdom. So, which kingdom will you support by your attitudes and behavior toward human imperfection? Will you be as I am—seeing with love and compassion? Or will you be as My enemy, decrying it, and condemning it? Will you hide it in shame and falsehood? Remember, My kingdom operates out of truth.

Will you speak as My enemy raising up a voice of judgment against yourself or others by countering My Word? Or will you move into My posture of bestowing grace out of compassion. Do you see the opportunities for new creations amidst the blemished? Open your eyes and see! Use My eyes, not yours.

It is given to Me alone to judge. As you issue forth judgments out of your own flesh, so shall they be heaped upon you. Evaluate between good and evil by using My Word and the direction of My Spirit. Turn away from evil absolutely! Do not ally yourself with those persons who are conducting evil. And yet, never stop loving them.

Never cease looking for opportunities to redeem and to heal by My power. Speak My Word. Do not surrender anyone into the enemy's camp. I alone have the authority to do this. Do not set about by your own flesh or understanding to try to remove blemishes from others or even from yourself. When discovered, release them into My keeping. Release them into My hand for My healing touch.

Often the scratches, dents, and blemishes on an antique piece endear it all the more to people's hearts. They say to your soul, "This precious thing has suffered much, it has been much loved, and it has endured in spite of frailty."

This is how I see My own. I see the journey. I see the lineage and the legacy of pain and pattern. Never forget, while I am the Creator, I am the Restorer, also. I do not demand perfection of My children before I love them. Neither should you demand that of yourself or of others in order for you or them to be worthy of love.

It is written that My grace is sufficient for you, and surely that is so. Then why do My children claim to need more? Why do they demand more when they are faced with that which is imperfect?

Receive My grace. Open yourself up to receive it from Me. Then, behold the new thing that shall arise in you. Its name is *grace*. It shall flow from My heart to your receptive heart. Then it shall flow from your heart to others. All the world shall see which kingdom you serve. As I love you, with all of your blemishes, so shall love arise in you, to hold the blemishes of others in compassion.

The
sheep hear
the voice
of their
Shepherd.
They
follow
Him,
finding
comfort in
His presence.
Seeing
truth in
His eyes,
they trust.
In Him
is
all truth.

WRITING THIS BOOK
A MESSAGE FROM THE AUTHOR

Many times I have been asked how it is that I can hear the whispers of the Shepherd of Israel. Some doubt that it is possible to hear Him clearly/purely, because of the clamor of our own human thoughts. Others doubt that He continues to speak; having chosen to discontinue engaging with us after the Bible was formed. My answer is found in the truth that He is constantly speaking...being "the same yesterday, today and forever." He spoke to the Jewish patriarchs, and to all who would listen since ancient days. He deeply wants us to know Him. The Scriptures clearly tell us that we only need to seek Him to discover Him. The Torah (Deuteronomy 4:9), the prophets (Jeremiah 29:12-14), and the New Covenant (Matthew 7:7-8) all tell us that if we seek God, we will find Him. What we find is a God who is neither mute, nor one who is watching us from a distance. He is still shepherding and He is still teaching us, Spirit to spirit. We only need to seek His presence, and linger there to hear His voice. If we become silent before Him, the still small voice becomes audible. The Scriptures speak also of the heart of our God...of the One who is always actively seeking us, so that His people might come to know Him personally.

I know this as a reality in my own life. At three years of age He began to seek me. It was then that I first began to love Him and to hear Him. Before my little mind and heart knew of Him, He sought me and revealed His great love for me at such a tender age. I remember the moment when I placed a small ring on my finger and pledged my love to Him. I still have that ring, locked away in a safe place. Knowing Him laid a foundation of faith and identity that has both established me and sustained me throughout a half century of life.

During a 40-day-fast in 1995, the Shepherd whispered that He would be sending me to Jerusalem—to the homeland of my Jewish people—to write for Him. I heard in His commission the cry of His heart; desiring to be known by His people. Within three days, the doors opened without effort, placing into my hands an airplane ticket, and living arrangements enabling me to venture out for the first time to the land of Abraham, Isaac, and Jacob. Each day I would arise to walk through a specific area of Jerusalem. I was not to write, but only to observe. Then each night, between 11 P.M. and 2 A.M., I would sit and await His word concerning what I had seen.

SWALLOWS AND SWIFTS were the outcome of a commanded visit to the Wailing Wall at dusk. POOLS AND POPPIES emerged from resting at the Pool of Bethesda at exactly 4 P.M., as the sun angled down upon the brilliant flowers. REFLECTIONS came to my heart after it was broken by a visit to Yad Va'Shem, the Holocaust museum. Each parable was the result of an appointed visit to observe, to listen, and to rest. Only later would the unfolding parable be whispered into my spirit, to be written down.

It is very important to me that my name be kept away from this writing, so that real author might have His voice heard—so that He might be made known to those who would choose to listen. It is also important for every reader to know that the Shepherd is speaking constantly with a heart of love for each and every lamb. Too many of us have lost hope in knowing and being known by God. Too many have chosen to believe the lie that we are god, and that all which is knowable comes through our own minds. Such doubt and arrogance must be laid aside, so that we listen with the ears of attentive children.

I pray this writing, which is the first book in a trilogy, will deeply bless and encourage every reader. I pray that each reader will be stirred to know Him intimately, far beyond the pages of this book. I pray that every reader will be inspired to hear His whispers personally...and come to love their Shepherd, as He loves each lamb.

Note about the Cover Art

The cover of *Whispers of the Shepherd* was produced through revelation given to a very gifted artist, Barbara A. Leone. Only one who seeks the face of the Shepherd is ever able to sketch such impressions from out of the Spirit.

Prayerfully seeking the inspiration for this book cover, Barbara waited to receive what would be given to her. The image appeared to her mind and she quickly reproduced it onto paper. What she did not realize at the time was the fact that the image was mysteriously embedded with hidden pictures. The profile of a lion, a nail, a dove, an eagle's claw-these are just a few of the hidden images within the larger art. Turning the cover sideways and upside down will reveal many surprising gifts, hidden within the lines and angles of this artwork. Enjoy the beauty and enjoy the treasure hunt.

THOUGHTS & REFLECTIONS

Additional copies of this book and other
book titles from DESTINY IMAGE are
available at your local bookstore.

Call toll-free: 1-800-722-6774.

Send a request for a catalog to:

Destiny Image® Publishers, Inc.

P.O. Box 310
Shippensburg, PA 17257-0310

*"Speaking to the Purposes of God for This
Generation and for the Generations to Come"*

For a complete list of our titles,
visit us at www.destinyimage.com